F3H DEMON
in detail & scale

+ SCALE SERIES
VOLUME 1
PRINT EDITION

by Bert Kinzey
Art by Rock Roszak

TABLE OF CONTENTS

Introduction	3
Developmental History	5
F3H Line Drawings	10
Demon Variants	
XF3H-1 Prototypes	12
F3H-1N (F-3A)	15
F3H-2N (F-3C)	19
F3H-2M (MF-3B)	24
F3H-2 (F-3B)	27
Demon Pilots' Report -- Demon Daze	30
A Demon Restoration	36
Demon Details	
Cockpit Details	39
Windscreen and Canopy Details	43
Fuselage Details	44
Wing Details	50
Pylons, Missile Rails, & External Stores	56
Landing Gear Details	60
Tail Details	66
Engine Details	69
Demon Squadrons Gallery	70
Atlantic Fleeet Squadrons	71
Pacific Fleet Squadrons	78
Test and Evaluation Squadrons	91
Modelers Section	93

COPYRIGHT 2018 BY DETAIL & SCALE

All rights reserved. No part of this publication may be reproduced in any form or transmitted by any means, electronic, mechanical, or otherwise without the expressed written consent of Detail & Scale.

This publication is a product of Detail & Scale which has sole responsibility for its content and layout, except that all contributors are responsible for the security clearance and copyright release of all materials they submit.

CONTRIBUTORS AND SOURCES

Jim Rotramel	Jim Mesko	Bob Bartolacci	Len Kaine	Jim Dorsey
Dick Koch	Bill Chaney	Lloyd Jones	Tommy Thomason	Ray Leader
David W. Menard	Don Spering	Don Linn	John Fox	John Loner
U. S. Navy	McDonnell Douglas	National Archives	National Naval Aviation Museum	
Grumman History Center		National Museum of the U. S. Air Force		Intrepid Sea, Air, and Space Museum

Detail & Scale expresses a special word of thanks to Hill Goodspeed and the staff at the National Naval Aviation Museum for their patience and outstanding support during the research and production of this publication. Many of the historic photographs came from their outstanding collection, and most of the detail photos were taken of their restored F3H-2M Demon. Without the cooperation and support of the National Naval Aviation Museum, this publication would not have been possible.

ISBN: 978-1-9804530-7-9

Between 1979 and 2004, Detail & Scale produced three series of books on U. S. military aircraft. Primary among these was the Detail & Scale Series which was the first series of aviation publications to focus on the details of aircraft, including the cockpits, radars, armament, powerplants, landing gear, and avionics/electronics systems. After six early monographs in this series, sixty-nine larger volumes followed, each extensively covering a specific American military aircraft from the World War II era to the present day. Each title also had a section in the back for scale modelers that reviewed the existing model kits available for the aircraft being covered by that book. The series became extremely popular with aviation enthusiasts as well as scale modelers.

In 2004, the series ended when Bert Kinzey, the owner of Detail & Scale, had to stop producing the books due to health reasons, and no new titles in the Detail & Scale Series were published between 2004 and 2013. In 2013, with advancements in digital technology, the opportunity presented itself for Detail & Scale to begin producing this detailed reference series on U. S. military aircraft as digital e-publications. In collaboration with Rock Roszak, the extensive Detail & Scale collection of photographs and reference material, collected for more than forty years, began being used to create reference publications in digital formats for military aviation enthusiasts.

The Detail & Scale Series of digital publications focuses on the details of military aircraft, just as the seventy-five printed volumes did for thirty-five years, only they now provide even greater detail and more extensive coverage. The advances in e-publications software and the digitization of photographs allow much more color to be included when available, and more information, artwork, charts, and photographs can be incorporated than the old printed book format, all at a much lower cost to the reader.

Detail & Scale has added new titles to the digital series that feature aircraft never included in any of the previous seventy-five printed books. We have also taken some of the popular printed books, updated and expanded them, and released them as digital publications.

In 2017, expanding capabilities began to make it possible for these digital publications to also become available in printed form through what is called "print-on-demand," for readers who prefer the printed format. The first new digital Detail & Scale book was published in early 2014 on the F3H Demon, which had originally been planned as the next book in the series when the series was suspended in 2004. This slightly abridged version of that original work is now available as this printed book, bringing many of the benefits of the digital publication--more pages and more photographs, particularly in color, to this new print-on-demand option.

Our books are supplemented by photo sets and artwork that are posted on our website at www.detailandscale.com. There, aviation enthusiasts will find photographs and artwork of many types of aircraft in addition to those covered in the Detail & Scale Series of print-on-demand books and e-publications.

Front Cover Photo: An F3H-2M Demon from the "Jolly Rogers" of VF-61 is spotted just forward of the superstructure aboard USS SARATOGA, CVA-60. Note that two of the pylons under the wing remain in the Sea Blue color, as does the launch rail on the white inboard pylon. By the time this photo was taken, the detachable inflight refueling probe had been added to the Demon. (National Naval Aviation Museum)

Rear Cover Photo: Although the Demon that is on display at the National Naval Aviation Museum was originally built as an F3H-2M, the restoration represents an F3H-2 assigned to the "Ghost Riders" of VF-193. The museum's restoration crew accurately restored the cockpit to the configuration used in the F3H-2N and F3H-2, and this included the large radar scope in the upper right section of the instrument panel. The earlier F3H-2M did not have this scope. Additional photographs showing the entire cockpit in this Demon can be found in the Demon Details chapter. (Kinzey)

INTRODUCTION

When this photograph of a Demon from VF-151 was taken aboard USS CORAL SEA, CVA-43, in 1963, the F3H-2 designation had been changed to F-3B. This was VF-151's second deployment aboard CORAL SEA while flying Demons, the first being two years earlier in 1961. Note that two upper 20-mm cannons have been removed and their gun ports covered over, leaving the aircraft with only the two lower cannons. This was a fairly common practice during the operational service of the F3H-2 variant of the Demon. (National Naval Aviation Museum)

When the Detail & Scale Series of books ended in 2004 after sixty-nine titles had been published, the next book planned was to be on the McDonnell F3H Demon. In 2013, the research and photography done in preparation for that book was used as the basis for the first digital publication in the Detail & Scale Series, and what was to be included in the previously planned printed edition was expanded considerably. The digital version of F3H Demon in Detail & Scale was released in 2013 and has been available ever since.

With emerging technologies used in producing publications, Detail & Scale is now able to also release this printed edition for readers who still prefer to have printed books. It also is much expanded over the previously planned publication, having more than 100 pages instead of only eighty. Further, the amount of color that is included is many times more extensive than it would have been originally. The latest technology allows us to use color throughout the book, rather than in a color section or only on certain pages, and to do so at a very reasonable price.

The F3H Demon, although plagued with a less than adequate powerplant, served the U. S. Navy as a night and all-weather fleet defense interceptor, a day fighter, and a fighter-bomber between 1956 and 1964. In McDonnell's line of "spooks," it was a step in between the straight-winged F2H Banshee, a first generation jet fighter for the Navy, and the far more powerful and supersonic F-4 Phantom II. All three of these aircraft, along with the FH-1 Phantom that preceded them, rolled off the production lines at the McDonnell Aircraft Corporation and onto the flight decks of the Navy's aircraft carriers.

This printed edition of **F3H Demon in Detail & Scale** follows the same format and basic layout of the digital version. Following this introduction, a developmental history is presented that covers the development of the various versions of the Demon and explains how the Demon fit into the rapidly changing advancements in carrier-borne jet fighter aircraft of the 1950s and early 1960s. This developmental history is followed by a chapter that takes a more detailed look at each Demon variant and the features that changed from one version to the next. Beginning with the XF3H-1 prototypes, each variant is looked at individually in more detail.

To add a personal look at the Demon right from its cockpit, a pilot's report is included by Len Kaine who flew the Demon during his service as a naval aviator. Len provides a prospective about the aircraft that can only come from someone who actually strapped into it and took it into the sky. His insight is a valuable addition to the coverage of the aircraft provided in this publication. In preparing his report, which he calls "Demon Daze," Len contacted several of his former squadron mates and added their recollections of the F3H to his own.

The next chapter takes a brief look at the restoration process of the National Naval Aviation Museum's beautifully restored Demon. This F3H-2M was painstakingly restored and painted in the markings of an F3H-2 from VF-193. It is one of only three Demons still in existence, and it is the one that is most extensively restored. It remains on display at the museum aboard NAS Pensacola, and it was photographed in detail for this publication.

As has always been the case with titles in the Detail & Scale Series of aviation publications, a major focus of this title is an extensive chapter covering the details of the aircraft. In the chapter on Demon details, dozens of photographs are included that extensively illustrate the cockpit and every external detail of the aircraft. Almost all of these photos were taken specifically for this publication to provide the most detailed coverage possible. From details inside the landing gear wells to the spoilers on top of the wings, and from the speed brakes to the arresting hook on the aft end of the fuselage, every feature is covered with detailed photography.

The next chapter takes a look at the Navy squadrons that flew the Demon. Included are photographs and artwork that illustrate the markings used by the various units. Extensive searches for relatively rare color photographs were made for this chapter, and Rock Roszak has nicely supplemented these photographs with artwork which depicts a wide range of markings from the simple to the most colorful ever applied to Demons.

One of the most popular features of the Detail & Scale Series of books for decades has been the Modeler's Section. This is included with comments and photographs covering the available scale model kits of the F3H Demon. Scale modelers will find this very helpful, because the model kits of the Demon that are available have numerous inaccuracies. Fortunately, most are relatively easy to correct if the modeler is aware of what they are, and our reviews make this possible.

This publication would not have been possible without the generous help and assistance of a number of people. Detail & Scale extends a special word of thanks to Hill Goodspeed at the National Naval Aviation Museum for his assistance and cooperation. Many of the general photographs in this publication came from the Museum's files, and the detailed photography was done on the Museum's beautifully restored F3H-2M. Trips were also made to study and photograph the F3H-2N on display at the Intrepid Sea, Air, and Space Museum in New York City, and to the National Archives in College Park, Maryland. The help and cooperation of the staffs at those locations is also acknowledged and appreciated.

There are several unusual features on this Demon that was assigned to VF-124 just before the squadron was merged into VF-121. First, it has silver landing gear struts, and the entire inside surface of each landing gear door is painted red. Photographs show that a number of Demons had silver gear struts and red inside surfaces on the gear doors, but the standard was white gear struts and red edges to the inside of the doors. Also note the location of the white rectangle with DANGER stenciled in red. In most cases, this was located inside the intake warning chevron, but in this case it is forward of the chevron, and it is partially covered by the 0 and the 3 of the modex. The gun camera is mounted to the left of centerline rather than to the right as it was on most Demons. There is no ADF antenna under the nose. Instead, it has been repositioned further aft under the center of the fuselage. This indicates that this Demon is probably an F3H-2. Although not unusual but worth noting, all four guns have been removed from this aircraft, and the pylons carried are the types used for rocket pods and bombs rather than missiles. The ram air turbine (RAT) has been extended beneath the center fuselage. (Photo from the collection of Lloyd Jones)

DEVELOPMENTAL HISTORY

When the first of the two XF3H-1 prototypes was rolled out of the McDonnell Aircraft Corporation's plant in St. Louis, its design features illustrated that it was a huge step forward over first generation jet fighters when it came to aerodynamic advancements. Its sleek fuselage and swept-back wings and tail surfaces were radical changes when compared to the earlier designs. But while the design of the airframe was excellent, it would be plagued by an engine that never lived up to its promise and was a source of continuing problems for the program. (McDonnell photograph via the National Naval Aviation Museum)

Work on what would become the F3H Demon had begun back in early 1948 when the Navy requested proposals for a high performance jet fighter to the aviation industry. Six aircraft companies responded with eleven different proposals, and two designs were accepted for development to the prototype stage. One was for the Douglas XF4D-1 Skyray, and the other was for McDonnell's Design 58 which the Navy designated the XF3H-1. On September 30, 1949, McDonnell received the contract for two prototypes. Unlike the first generation fighters with their straight wings, the new design featured a leading edge sweep back of forty-five degrees at one-quarter chord, and the vertical and horizontal tail surfaces were also swept back. It should be noted that when the XF3H-1 prototypes were ordered, it was envisioned that the aircraft would be a high-performance day fighter, however the change to meet the night-fighting requirement would be made prior to the first production order.

With work on the FH-1 Phantom and F2H Banshee well underway, and with expected additional orders for the production F3H-1Ns, the future of McDonnell Aircraft looked very bright. McDonnell would soon bestow the name, Demon, on the aircraft making it the third "spook" in its continuing line of jet fighters for the Navy.

Unlike the Phantom and the Banshee, the Demon was to be powered by only one engine. The Navy specified that the engine would be the Westinghouse J40, a very promising design that offered considerably more thrust than the jet engines then in service. But this choice of engine would prove to be completely unsatisfactory, and it almost spelled disaster for the entire project.

Originally, the J40-WE-8 was chosen for the two XF3H-1 prototypes, but its development was plagued with problems and delays. The more powerful J40-WE-10 was then selected, but problems with it delayed its availability as well. As a temporary measure, the non-afterburning version, the J40-WE-6, was fitted to the prototype so that flight testing could begin, and even then the maiden flight of the first XF3H-1, BuNo. 125444, did not take place until August 7, 1951, with Robert M. Edholm at the controls. The early flight tests confirmed what was already known. The J40-WE-6 left the XF3H-1 significantly and even dangerously underpowered.

After more delays with the J40 powerplant that held up the program, McDonnell recommended to the Navy that another engine be selected for the Demon. But for the time being, the Navy stayed with the J40 as Westinghouse developed the J40-WE-22 and then the J40-WE-22A for the production F3H-1Ns. By January 1952, the second XF3H-1 prototype, BuNo. 125445, had joined the first in flight testing. The problems with the engine were not simply a lack of power. Testing also indicated that it was very unreliable, particularly at high altitudes.

Finally, in January 1953, the J40-WE-8 with its afterburner was considered ready for flight testing, and the first flight was made with the more powerful engine. It proved to be problematic, causing groundings and more delays to the program.

Carrier suitability trials with the second of the XF3H-1 prototypes began in August 1953 aboard USS CORAL SEA, CVA-43, but the lingering problems with the engine delayed them as well. Interestingly, the XF4D-1 Skyray was aboard the carrier conducting carrier trials at the same time. Except for the engine problems, the Demon exhibited no significant difficulties operating from a carrier. Some visibility issues during carrier approaches were noted, and these would be addressed on the production aircraft.

The first prototype experienced a fuel explosion on March 9, 1954. The pilot ejected, but the aircraft was destroyed. This

5

The engine is started on the second of the two XF3H-1 prototypes during carrier qualifications aboard USS CORAL SEA, CVA-43, in August 1953. Note the triangular shaped auxiliary air inlet door is rotated ninety degrees, allowing additional air into the inlet duct as the engine is started. The Westinghouse J40 powerplant continued to be a problem during the carrier qualifications and delayed their completion, but otherwise the Demon proved to be very well suited for carrier operations. (Official U. S. Navy photograph via the National Naval Aviation Museum)

The F3H-1N was the first production version of the Demon to be ordered. But serious problems with the Westinghouse J40-WE-10 engine resulted in several early crashes. The Navy canceled the order after only fifty-six F3H-1Ns were delivered. While some of these flew with test units for a brief period of time, they were soon grounded, and none were ever assigned to operational fleet squadrons. (Official U. S. Navy photograph via the National Naval Aviation Museum)

brought the test program to an end. The second prototype was grounded and eventually scrapped.

When the Navy initially issued the contract for the two XF3H-1 prototypes, it envisioned the aircraft as an advanced clear-air day fighter. But as time went on, the successful development of other day fighters led to operational service for several types. The Navy realized that there was a greater need for an advanced night-capable interceptor that would replace the F2H-3 and F2H-4 Banshees. Accordingly, the requirements for the first production Demons were changed to meet this need, and the designation for these aircraft was changed to F3H-1N. This brought back the historic "N" suffix for night fighter that dated back to the night fighting Hellcats of World War II. To provide the eyes for the night capability, the nose of the Demon was enlarged to house an APD-50 radar.

McDonnell received a contract for 150 F3H-1Ns in March 1951 in spite of the continuing serious problems with the J40 engine. The Navy specified that the J40-WE-8, used in the prototypes, be replaced with the more powerful J40-WE-10 in the F2H-1Ns. But this version of the J40 was larger and heavier, and the fuselage had to be redesigned to accommodate it. Internal fuel capacity was increased, and the manual wing fold mechanism of the prototypes was replaced by a hydraulic wing folding system on the production aircraft. The cockpit and nose section was angled down five degrees, and a larger frameless windscreen replaced the framed design of the prototypes to provide better visibility, particularly during carrier landings. This would also cause problems and would later be replaced with a framed windscreen.

On December 24, 1953, the first F3H-1N made its initial flight, and the seriousness of the engine problems became painfully clear. In a very short period of time, Demons were involved in eight crashes which killed four pilots and completely destroyed six aircraft. The Navy had no choice but to ground the Demon and halt production after only fifty-six F3H-1Ns were completed. No F3H-1Ns ever entered service with an operational fleet squadron.

There was little question that the Demon was a good design that offered considerable potential. The problem was the Westinghouse J40 engine. It had caused lengthy delays in the program, and its problems had never been solved. To save the aircraft from disaster, the Navy decided to replace the J40 with the Allison J71-A-2, something McDonnell had been requesting for some time. Two F3H-1Ns were fitted with the Allison powerplant and flown as test aircraft with success. Another two were upgraded to F2H-2N standards to serve as prototypes for what would become the next production version of the aircraft. While the J71 still did not provide the Demon with as much power as desired, it was more than the J40, and although the J71 had some problems of its own, it was far more reliable than the J40.

To handle the added weight of the F2H-2N, the wing area was increased from 442 to 519 square feet. This was accomplished without increasing the span. Instead, the root cord was extended aft by forty inches, and the new trailing edge from that point was

The first version of the Demon to become operational with Navy squadrons was the F3H-2N. This variant was powered by the Allison J71-A-2 engine, and the fuselage and wings had major design changes compared to the previous F3H-1N. They were also delivered in the Light Gull Gray over white paint scheme. These F3H-2Ns were assigned to VF-141 and photographed aboard USS SHANGRI-LA, CVA-38, during the carrier's 1958-1959 cruise. (Official U. S. Navy photograph via the National Naval Aviation Museum)

tapered out to the original wing tip. The AN/APQ-50 radar of the F3H-1N was replaced with the AN/APG-51A. The capability to employ the AAM-N-7A (later redesignated AIM-9B) Sidewinder, infrared-homing, air-to-air missile was included. A total of 142 F3H-2Ns were delivered, and the Demon finally entered service with operational fleet squadrons in 1956.

While the F3H-2N was a night fighter and could employ the infrared-guided Sidewinder air-to-air missile, the Navy wanted to further increase the capabilities of the aircraft. At the time the Demon was entering service, the development of radar guided missiles was reaching a point where they could be added to the air-to-air armament carried by interceptors. To take advantage of this new weapon, the Navy ordered that the F3H-2M version of the Demon be developed concurrently with the F3H-2N. The F3H-2M was designed to employ the AAM-N-2 Sparrow I missile. The AAM-N-2 used a beam-riding guidance system, meaning it guided along a beam generated by the radar in the aircraft. A total of 80 F3H-2Ms were delivered to the Navy, however the Sparrow I missile proved to be highly unreliable, and it was seldom, if ever, employed operationally with fleet squadrons aboard carriers.

Although extensive testing was conducted with the Sparrow I on the Demon and other aircraft such as the F3D Skyknight, the beam riding guidance system did not prove to be as effective as desired. Instead, another form of radar guidance, known as semi-active homing, proved to be the far better option. With this guidance system, the interceptor's radar illuminated the target, and the missile's own radar receiver homed in on the reflected radar energy from the target. This system was used on the AAM-N-6 (later AIM-7C) Sparrow III missile, and it would be this version of the Sparrow that would become operational with fleet squadrons in great numbers.

To utilize the Sparrow III, the Demon's radar had to be upgraded. The new version of the radar was designated AN/APQ-51B. This was installed in the final and definitive Demon variant, the F3H-2. (Note that there was no letter suffix after the -2.) This made the F3H-2 a true all-weather interceptor, capable of finding targets at any time, day or night, and in any weather conditions. Once found, the targets could be engaged with both guns and missiles.

The second variant of the Demon to go into service with Navy squadrons was the F3H-2M, which could employ the AAM-N-2 Sparrow I air-to-air missile. The Sparrow I was a beam rider missile, meaning it rode a radar beam to its target. However, tests with the missile proved that it was very unreliable. This F3H-2M was assigned to the Navy test facility at Point Mugu, California, and is shown with a Sparrow I missile under its wing. (Official U. S. Navy photograph via the National Naval Aviation Museum)

F3H-2, BuNo. 145239, is positioned on Cat ONE aboard USS FRANKLIN D. ROOSEVELT, CVA-42, in February 1959. The Demon was assigned to the "Top Hatters" of VF-14 at that time. Note the Sidewinder missile on the underwing pylon. (National Naval Aviation Museum)

When the infrared-guided AAM-N-7A (later AIM-9B) Sidewinder air-to-air missile became available, it was used by all operational versions of the Demon. F3H-2s often carried two Sidewinders and two Sparrow IIIs to provide both infrared and radar guided missiles to deal with any threats they might encounter, but photographic evidence confirms that four Sparrow IIIs were also carried at times.

F3H-2s were delivered with what was known as a short beaver tail. Earlier Demons had a rather long, flat fuselage extension aft of the vertical and horizontal tails. This became known as the beaver tail. This extension was shortened by approximately two feet on the F3H-2.

As with any aircraft, several problems were noted during the Demon's operational life that were addressed with changes. Three of these are worthy of note. Soon after the F3H-2N became operational, it was discovered that applying hard aileron forces to induce high roll rates caused the wing to twist and warp. Rather than redesign a stronger and heavier wing structure, spoilers were added on top of the wings to spread the forces out across a larger area of the wing, and this solved the wing warping problem. F3H-2N and F3H-2Ms, originally delivered without the spoilers, had them retrofitted, and they were a production standard on the F3H-2 variant. Close-up photographs in the Demon Details section of this publication provide a detailed look at the wing spoilers.

The second major problem area was the ejection seat. As originally delivered, the Demon had an ejection seat designed by McDonnell. Its use had demonstrated that it was unreliable and unsafe. The Navy ordered a change to a new ejection seat designed by Martin Baker. This H5 seat became standard starting with the production of F3H-2, BuNo. 146709, which was the last production block of Demons delivered. It was retrofitted to earlier aircraft already in service. Both types of ejection seats are illustrated in the Demon Details Chapter.

The third problem had to do with the Allison J71-A-2 engine. It was found that the super-cooling of the engine in the very low temperatures at high altitudes would sometimes cause the shroud around the turbine blades to shrink in size to the point that it was too small in diameter for the turbine blades inside. This condition

MAIN DIFFERENCES TABLE

ITEM	F3H-2N	F3H-2M	F3H-2
SPOILERS	SOME AIRPLANES	SOME AIRPLANES	YES
RADAR	AN/APG-51A	AN/APQ-51A	AN/APQ-51B
TACAN	YES	PROVISIONS ONLY	YES
MISSILE CAPABILITY	SIDEWINDER	SPARROW I SIDEWINDER	SPARROW III SIDEWINDER
SELECTIVE IDENTIFICATION FEATURE	SOME AIRPLANES	SOME AIRPLANES	YES
BEAVER TAIL	LONG	LONG	SHORT

This table was adapted from one found in the NATOPS manual for the Demon. It shows the main differences between the three versions of the Demon that obtained operational status with U. S. Navy fleet squadrons. It should be noted that the only version of the Demon that could employ the Sparrow III missile was the F3H-2. Many publications and other sources state that the F3H-2M could carry the Sparrow III, but the radar in the F3H-2M was not capable of illuminating the target for the semi-active homing Sparrow III. Some F3H-2Ns were upgraded to F3H-2 standards and could employ the Sparrow III missile.

would cause an engine failure. To correct the problem, Allison shaved off the tips of the blades so that they would remain clear of the shroud even under such super-cooled conditions. But this reduced the power of the engine considerably, and the effective service ceiling of the Demon was substantially reduced.

The Demon entered service in operational fleet squadrons in 1956, when the "Top Hatters" of VF-14 transitioned to the F3H-2N. For eight years, it served in carrier air wings along with several different day fighters ranging from North American's FJ-3/4 Fury to Vought's F8U Crusader. During that time, it was the fleet's primary night-capable interceptor. With its AN/APQ-51B radar and Sparrow III capability, the F3H-2 version of the Demon stood ready to engage hostile airborne threats at any time and in any weather. Although the Demon could not be called an outstanding success, it could be considered adequate for the mission it was intended to perform. It was praised for its flying abilities but cursed for the engine that never let it live up to its full potential.

The Demon participated in some of the events of the Cold War that grabbed the headlines of its day. From Lebanon in the Mediterranean to the islands of Quemoy and Matsu in the Southwest Pacific, Demons flew missions ranging from covering U. S. troops on the ground to providing Combat Air Patrol (CAP) over the fleet. In 1962, Demon squadrons took part in the blockade during the Cuban Missile Crisis. All Demon squadrons are covered in the Demon Squadrons Gallery chapter of this publication. Photographs and artwork illustrate many of the various markings used by the squadrons during those deployments.

McDonnell developed several proposals for an improved Demon Variant. Most notable of these was the F3H-G and F3H-H, the former being powered by two General Electric J65 engines and the latter by two General Electric J79s. A wooden mockup was displayed at the McDonnell plant in 1954, but neither version was ever ordered even as a prototype. However, the design of the F3H-H would lay the groundwork for the F4H-1 (later F-4) Phantom that would ultimately replace the Demon as the Navy's primary all-weather interceptor as well as become a very capable and versatile fighter-bomber.

In 1962, the Department of Defense ordered a standardization of aircraft designations that would be uniform among all services. The new general designation for the Demon was F-3, but the additional prefixes and suffixes were misallocated and very confusing. Whether this was due to incompetence or by design has been lost

Throughout its service, the Demon served as the Navy's primary interceptor, sharing the flight decks and hangar bays of aircraft carriers with several different types of day fighters and fighter-bombers. In this photo, dated October 1961, F3H-2s of VF-141 are spotted along the port side of the flight deck aboard USS LEXINGTON, CVA-16, with F8U Crusader day fighters and FJ-4 Fury fighter-bombers. (Official U. S. Navy photograph via the National Naval Aviation Museum)

McDonnell proposed several improved Demon variants, but none made it to the flying prototype level of development. The wooden mock-up of the F3H-H is shown on display at the McDonnell plant. It led to the development of the highly successful F-4 Phantom II. (McDonnell photograph via the National Naval Aviation Museum)

The markings used by VF-21's Demons are displayed on F3H-2, BuNo. 143435. Note the treatment of the jet intake warning chevron on this aircraft. The white rectangle with the word DANGER in red is not used. Instead, DANGER is painted in white on both the upper and lower segments of the chevron along with JET INTAKE. The upper 20-mm cannons have been deleted, and their openings have been covered. The pallet for the ammunition cans is lowered behind the nose gear. An AERO 4A launcher for the Sparrow III missile is on the outboard wing pylon, and an AERO 1A launcher for the Sidewinder missile is on the inboard pylon. The face curtain handles at the top of the ejection seat indicate that this Demon has the Martin Baker H5 seat. (National Naval Aviation Museum)

to history. First, the XF3H-1 prototypes were given the designation XF-3A, even though neither airframe still existed. Likewise, the F3H-1N was redesignated F-3A, although none of them remained in the inventory in 1962. Under the new designation system, the letter suffix was intended to designate each variant of the aircraft alphabetically in chronological order. Since the Demon variants had entered service in the chronological order of F3H-2N, F3H-2M, and F3H-2, the proper designations for these variants under the new system should have been F-3B, F-3C, and F-3D, respectively. But this was not the case. The last variant to enter service, the F3H-2, was redesignated F-3B, while the F3H-2M became the MF-3B, as though it was somehow a sub-variant of the F-3H-2/F-3B, which it was not. The F3H-2N was redesignated the F-3C, even though it had entered service prior to the F-3B and MF-3B.

Additionally, BuNos. 133520 and 133522, which had served as prototypes for the F3H-2N, were redesignated YF-3Cs, and BuNo. 133569, the first of the F3H-2Ms, was redesignated YMF-3B. None of these three aircraft were still in service when the new standardized system of designations was put in place, so why they were provided with new designations remains a mystery.

For the purposes of this publication, we will use the original Navy designations to avoid confusion and having the reader need to remember which new designation went with which Demon variant.

In the early 1960s, the Demon began to be phased out of service as it was replaced by the Phantom. The last fleet squadron to fly the Demon was VF-161 at NAS Miramar, California. They made the final Demon flight by an operational squadron in September 1964 as they completed their transition to the F-4B Phantom. In addition to the fleet squadrons, VC-3, VX-3, and VX-4 operated Demons, however no Demons were ever assigned to Naval Reserve squadrons.

VF-161 was the last fleet squadron to fly the Demon before transitioning to the F-4 Phantom II in September 1964. By then the Demon had been redesignated the F-3, and the version flown by VF-161 was the F-3B, formerly designated the F3H-2. One of the Demons is shown here next to the aircraft that replaced it. Fittingly, it was the next "spook" fighter from McDonnell, the F-4B Phantom II. (Photo from the collection of the National Naval Aviation Museum)

F3H-2N/-2M/-2 LINE DRAWINGS

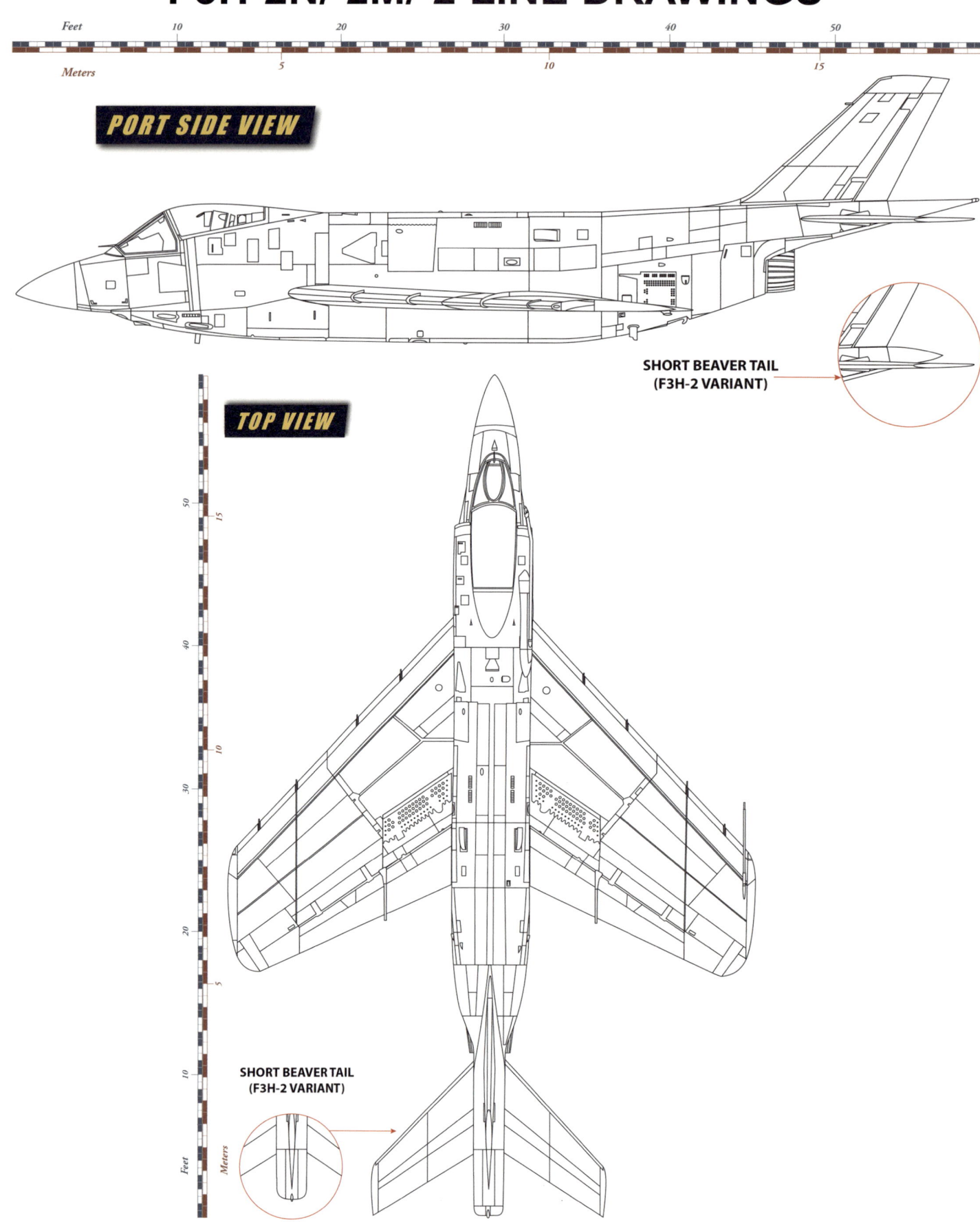

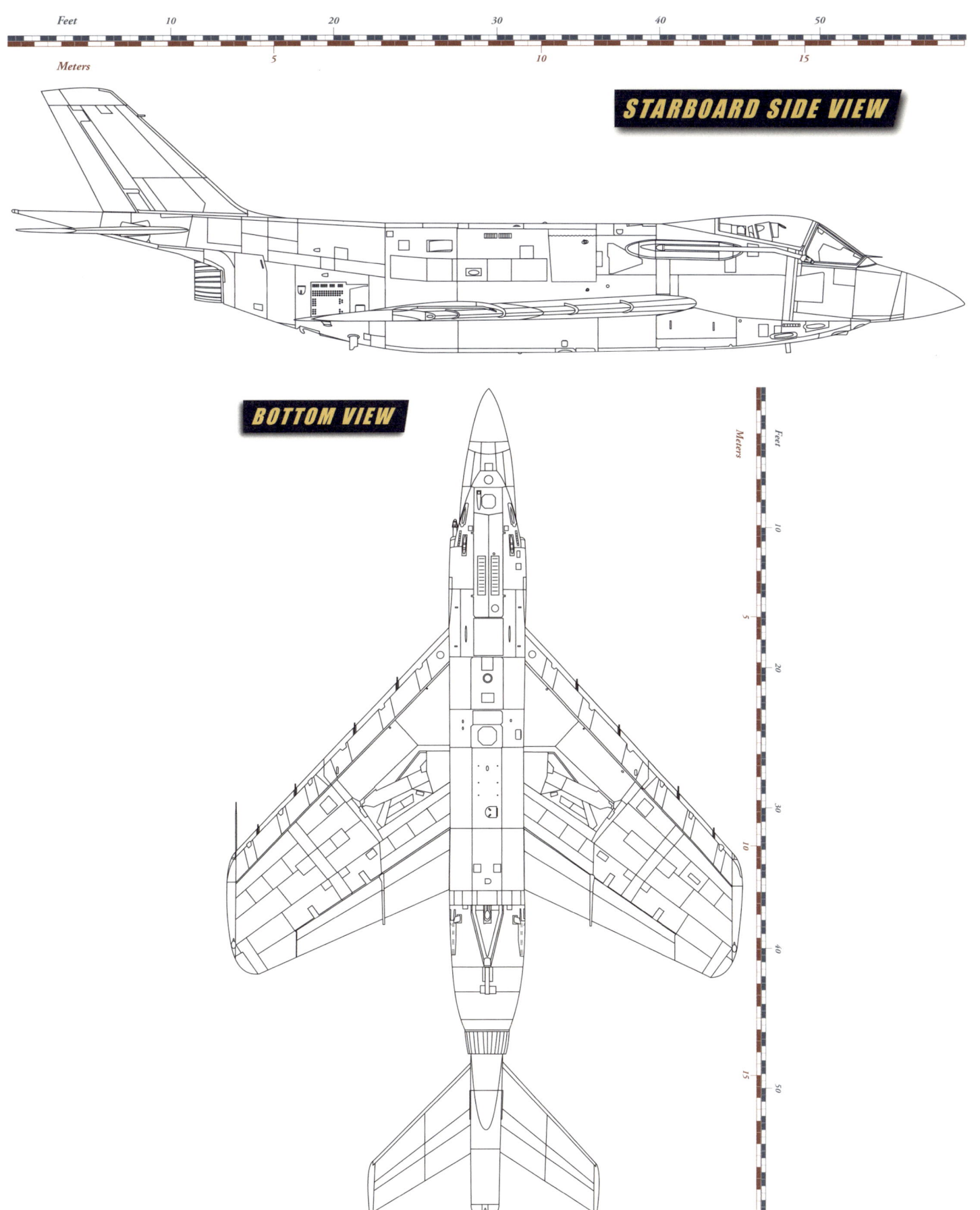

DEMON VARIANTS
XF3H-1 PROTOTYPES

A very rare color photograph of one the Demon prototypes shows the second XF3H-1, BuNo. 125445, while it was undergoing its carrier suitability evaluation aboard USS CORAL SEA, CVA-43. The aircraft is about to be towed off of the Number TWO elevator, and the fact that the triangular-shaped auxiliary inlet doors are open indicates that the engine is idling. (Official U. S. Navy photograph via the National Naval Aviation Museum)

On September 30, 1949, The Navy issued a contract to the McDonnell Aircraft Corporation for two prototypes of an advanced, swept-wing, jet fighter design which the Navy designated XF3H-1. Bureau Numbers 125444 and 125445 were assigned to the two aircraft. As originally ordered, the XF3H-1 was intended to be a high-performance day fighter, but before the first production aircraft were ordered, the requirement changed to a night fighter.

By the time the contract was issued for the prototypes in 1949, both McDonnell and the Navy had gained experience with first generation jet fighters, with McDonnell having moved from producing the FH-1 Phantom to the F2H Banshee. Deliveries of the F2H-1s had been completed, and the production line had changed over to the F2H-2 variant that would be produced in considerable numbers for use by both the Navy and Marines. Three sub-variants of the F2H-2 would be produced and see extensive use, operating from aircraft carriers and land bases during the Korean War. But the XF3H-1 was to be radically different from any of the early jets. Gone were the straight wings and tail surfaces of the previous designs. Instead, the wings were swept back forty-five degrees at one-quarter chord, and both the horizontal and vertical tail surfaces were also swept back as advancements in aerodynamics paved the way for sleeker designs to achieve even greater speeds than their predecessors.

McDonnell had designed both the Phantom and Banshee with two engines buried in the wing roots. But the new fighter would have a single powerplant in the fuselage, and while this design change was not consequential in and of itself, the engine chosen for the aircraft proved to have severe and continuing problems, which almost doomed the program. The Navy specified that the Westinghouse J40-WE-8 turbojet was to be used in the XF3H-1, but Westinghouse never successfully solved the many problems with the engine, and its use would eventually have to be abandoned.

It should be noted that the Navy had also issued a contract for a new fighter to Douglas on the very same day as the XF3H-1 contract was given to McDonnell, and it would take the form of

The first XF3H-1 prototype, BuNo. 125444, was rolled out of the McDonnell plant in early 1951. From this angle, the swept wings and tail surfaces are visible as is the sleek design of the fuselage. Note also the lack of an afterburner nozzle protruding from the fuselage. This was because the aircraft initially had to be fitted with the Westinghouse J40-WE-6 engine which did not have an afterburner. (McDonnell photograph via the National Archives)

XF3H-1 Number One is shown here on an early test flight, still fitted with the J40-WE-6 engine without an afterburner. When this photograph was taken, the aircraft was in slow flight with the leading edge slats and the flaps extended. Note also that the auxiliary inlet door is open at this slow speed. (McDonnell photograph via the National Archives)

The left side of the first XF3H-1 is illustrated in this view taken during the early taxi tests. When sitting on its landing gear, the Demon had a pronounced nose high attitude. (McDonnell photograph via the National Naval Aviation Museum)

the F4D Skyray. While McDonnell was working on the XF3H-1, Douglas was developing the XF4D-1, and the Navy had specified that the Westinghouse J40 be used to power both fighters. Knowing the problems Westinghouse was having with the J40, Douglas designed the XF4D-1 so that it could easily accept a jet engine of a different size and design should the J40 prove to be a failure. McDonnell did not do the same for the XF3H-1, and this lack of foresight would cause a major redesign effort to save the Demon when the J40 engine had to be changed to the Allison J71. By comparison, Douglas was able to change to the Pratt & Whitney J57 with little difficulty or delay, and it proved to be a very powerful and reliable powerplant for the production F4D-1 Skyrays.

Designed by McDonnell's Richard Deagen, the first XF3H-1 prototype, BuNo. 125444, was completed and rolled out of the plant at St. Louis in early 1951. Its very appearance dramatized the fact that it was a giant step forward in aircraft design over the previous Phantom and Banshee. Even sitting on the ground, the sleek aircraft with its pointed nose and swept wings and tail surfaces looked like it was going Mach 1. It offered the promise of a significant increase in performance that would be on a par or even exceed that of the Air Force's F-86 Sabre which was already in service. Unlike the twin-engined FH-1 Phantom and F2H Banshee before it, its design called for a single jet engine. Given that the F-4 Phantom and F-101 Voodoo that followed it both had two engines, the Demon would remain the only single engine jet fighter ever put into production by McDonnell.

Although the aircraft was ready to fly, Westinghouse was unable to deliver the J40-WE-8 engine to power the aircraft. The Navy had changed the powerplant to the more powerful J40-WE-10 for production F3H-1Ns, but this too was not ready to be installed in the prototype. After more delays, it was decided that the prototype would temporarily be fitted with the J40-WE-6 engine so that some flight testing could begin. Unlike the -8 and -10 versions of the J40, the -6 did not have an afterburner, and it could produce only 6,500 pounds of thrust. Early photographs of the prototypes, taken when the -6 version of the engine was fitted, are distinguishable because of the absence of an afterburner convergent/divergent nozzle protruding from the fuselage.

Taxi tests were conducted starting in July of 1951, and were soon followed by the maiden flight of twenty-four minutes by the first prototype, BuNo. 125444, on August 7. Early flight testing clearly illustrated that the J40-WE-6 engine left the Demon significantly and even dangerously underpowered, however the aircraft proved to be very easy to fly. It was maneuverable and the controls were positive and responsive. It flew well at all speeds and configurations except at high altitudes where the reliability problems with the engine became even worse. To improve handling characteristics at the higher altitudes, design changes were made

The second XF3H-1, BuNo. 125445, flew for more than a year before the J40-WE-8 powerplant with its afterburner was finally ready to be installed. The convergent-divergent nozzle of the afterburner is visible extending from the fuselage in this view. Also note the name, Demon, painted on the nose. (McDonnell photograph via the National Archives)

This early photo of the second XF3H-1 prototype clearly shows the thinner fuselage of the prototypes and the more pointed nose. Also note the boundary layer fence on the wing. The boundary layer fences were originally fitted to the prototypes, but they would be deleted by the time this aircraft conducted the carrier suitability trials aboard USS CORAL SEA. Compare this photograph to the ones of the same aircraft that were taken during those trials. (McDonnell photograph from the collection of Don Spering)

XF3F-1, BuNo. 125445, taxis forward on the flight deck of USS CORAL SEA, CVA-43, during carrier suitability trials in August 1953. NAVY was lettered on both sides of the vertical tail for these trials. (Official U. S. Navy photograph via the National Naval Aviation Museum)

At the same time the second Demon prototype was conducting carrier suitability trials, one of the Douglas XF4D-1 Skyray prototypes was also undergoing its carrier evaluations. Here the two aircraft pass each other on the flight deck. Both fighters were originally to be powered by the Westinghouse J40 engine, but when its severe problems could not be solved, a different powerplant was chosen for each of the two aircraft. Production versions of the Skyray would be powered by the Pratt & Whitney J57, while the Demon, starting with the F3H-2N version, would be fitted with the Allison J71. (Official U. S. Navy photograph via the National Naval Aviation Museum)

to the control surfaces. The Navy was pleased with the aircraft, and remained confident enough in the engine to confirm an order for 150 F3H-1N night fighters that had been placed with McDonnell in March even before the taxi tests had begun. An order for an additional 100 aircraft to be built by Temco was also issued.

With the Korean War being fought on the other side of the globe, the desire to get the new aircraft into production was intensified, especially when the swept-wing MiG-15 made its appearance and proved to be superior to any of the Navy's existing jet fighters. This also made the delays caused by the engine problems all the more frustrating. The second XF3H-1, BuNo. 125445, did not make its first flight until January 1952, and it was also initially fitted with the non-afterburning J40-WE-6 engine, because there was still no version of the J40 with an afterburner available. In April, McDonnell recommended to the Navy that a replacement engine be found and suggested that the Allison J71 with an afterburner be considered. The Navy refused to make the change, and it would be yet another year before the first flight by one of the prototypes equipped with the J40-WE-8 engine and its afterburner.

The entire year of 1952 was a series of fits and starts with the two prototypes. Plagued with a severely underpowered and unreliable engine, there was only so much that could be gained from the flight testing. Both McDonnell and the Navy realized they had an aircraft with considerable potential if only the engine problems could be solved.

Both of the XF3H-1 prototypes remained in a natural metal finish throughout their entire existence. During the 1950s, prototypes of Navy jet fighters flew with several different paint schemes. While many were painted in overall Gloss Sea Blue, the standard for U. S. carrier-based aircraft of the day, some were natural metal like the Demon. Grumman's XF9F-2 Panther and XF11F Tiger were natural metal, and for a while an XF4D-1 Skyray also sported a natural metal finish. Other prototypes were painted overall gloss white, but not the XF3H-1s. When the second prototype joined the flight testing, the name, Demon, had been bestowed on the aircraft, and it was added to both sides of the nose in black letters.

Finally, in January 1953, a year after the second XF3H-1 prototype had begun flight testing, the first flight with the J40-WE-8 engine and its afterburner took place. With this version of the powerplant installed, the afterburner's convergent/divergent nozzle extended beyond the opening in the lower rear fuselage. However, it was quickly apparent that even with the afterburner, the aircraft was still significantly underpowered and could not come anywhere close to reaching its design potential. Major reliability problems surfaced that resulted in a number of groundings causing further delays with the program. Still, the Navy refused to change to a different engine. More design changes were made to the wings in an attempt to solve the continuing high altitude handling issues.

In August 1953, carrier suitability trials with the second XF3H-1 began, but the problems with the engine delayed these as well, and they were not completed until October. Other than the insufficient power and reliability factors of the J40-WE-8, the carrier suitability trials, which were conducted aboard USS CORAL SEA, CVA-43, indicated no major problems with the Demon when it came to operating aboard an aircraft carrier. The only noteworthy change that was indicated involved a lack of visibility while flying the approach to landing, and as a result the windscreen was redesigned and the cockpit and nose was angled down five degrees on production aircraft. Ironically, at the same time the second XF3H-1 was conducting carrier trials aboard USS CORAL SEA, one of the Douglas XF4D-1 Skyrays was aboard flying suitability trials as well. Like the Demon, it had been delayed by the troublesome J40 engine.

Flight testing with the two prototypes continued until March 9, 1954, when the first XF3H-1 experienced an engine explosion and crashed. McDonnell test pilot, Gilbert North, ejected at 15,000 feet. The second prototype was immediately grounded and was eventually scrapped. Only nine days after the crash of the first prototype, one of the early production F2H-1Ns experienced an engine fire and crashed. The Demon was in production, but the problems were far from over, and it would still be a long time before it would become operational with Navy squadrons.

F3H-1N (F-3A)

The first two production F3H-1Ns, BuNos. 133489 and 133490, were used as test and evaluation aircraft. BuNo. 133891, shown here, became the first F3H-1N delivered to full production standards without the instrumentation probes. Note the lowered nose section with the large, one-piece windscreen. This change from the prototypes was made to improve visibility during approach to landing aboard aircraft carriers. This Demon was destroyed in a crash on November 1, 1954. (Official U. S. Navy photograph via Tommy Thomason)

When the Navy placed the order for the two XF3H-1 prototypes, it planned for the aircraft to be a high performance day fighter. But the decision was soon made to make the Demon a night fighter equipped with a radar to permit it to carry out intercepts in all weather conditions and at night. To reflect this mission capability, the Navy added the "N" suffix to the designation assigned to the first production variant of the Demon, the F3H-1N. The radar required a larger nose section with a radome to house the antenna and its associated equipment. Provisions were made for the AN/APQ-50 radar in the first thirty aircraft, although it was never fitted. But the larger nose would be only one of several design changes required for the F3H-1N.

During carrier trials aboard USS CORAL SEA, CVA-43, with the second XF3H-1, the forward visibility was found to be marginal while flying the approach to landing. To remedy this problem, the nose of the aircraft, including the cockpit, was angled down five degrees. The F3H-1N was also fitted with a larger one-piece windscreen design, but this would prove problematic and would later be replaced with a framed windscreen. The manually folding wings of the prototypes were replaced with hydraulic folding wings on the F3H-1N.

The most significant and noticeable design changes were related to the troublesome J40 engine. The Navy chose the J40-WE-22 to replace the J40-WE-8 that was finally installed in the two XF3H-1s. The J40-WE-22 produced 6,500 pounds of thrust in normal power, 7,250 pounds in military power, and 10,900 pounds in afterburner. While this was an improvement over the J40-WE-8, it still left the Demon considerably underpowered. But more thrust meant higher fuel consumption, so internal fuel capacity was increased. This was accomplished by enlarging the fuselage, making it deeper than that of the XF3H-1 prototypes. The F3H-1N could carry 1,202 gallons of fuel in its three fuselage tanks and another 304 gallons in four fuel tanks mounted inside the wings. The J40-WE-22 also required more air to mix with the fuel, so the

A Westinghouse J40 engine is on display at the National Naval Aviation Museum in Pensacola, Florida. It was the critical and ongoing problems with this powerplant that almost caused the demise of the Demon program, and its failure resulted in the end of jet engine production at Westinghouse. The interesting cutaway display at the Museum reveals the complex details of the powerplant. (Both, Kinzey)

The first production F3H-1N, BuNo. 133489, is shown during an early test flight. Note the long instrumentation probe on the nose. F3H-1Ns had their standard pitot probes mounted under the nose. (McDonnell photograph via the National Naval Aviation Museum)

air inlets were enlarged, and the triangular-shaped auxiliary air inlet doors were moved further aft.

The Navy placed an order for 150 F3H-1Ns in March of 1951, and the mock-up was inspected and approved in July of that year. But lingering problems with the Westinghouse engine caused lengthy delays, and the first flight did not take place until December of 1953. The first two F3H-1Ns, BuNos. 133489 and 133490, were fitted with instrumentation probes and served as test and evaluation aircraft.

While the first two F3H-1Ns conducted test flights, additional aircraft continued to roll off the production lines at the McDonnell plant in St. Louis. At that time the Navy's standard paint scheme for carrier-based aircraft was overall Gloss Sea Blue, and the F3H-1Ns were painted in this scheme. The leading edges of all flying surfaces were painted with silver Corogard, and all stenciling was in white.

Although major problems with the J40 continued, flight testing demonstrated that the Demon was very maneuverable and had

The second production F3H-1N, BuNo. 133490, was also used for testing. It is shown here in slow flight with the landing gear retracted, but the leading edge slats are forward. In addition to the instrumentation probe on the nose, there is another long probe on the left wing tip. On later production Demons, a static pressure probe would be located on the right wing tip. (McDonnell photograph via the National Naval Aviation Museum)

When problems continued with the Westinghouse J40 engine, two F3H-1Ns, BuNos. 133519 and 133521 were used to evaluate the Demon with the Allison J71 turbojet. BuNo. 133519 is shown here while being used to test the J71. (McDonnell photograph via Jim Mesko)

excellent flying qualities. Ordnance testing was conducted at the Naval Air Test Center at NAS Patuxent River, Maryland, and no problems were encountered with weapons delivery or separation from the aircraft. Armament for the F3H-1N included four 20-mm cannon in the lower fuselage beneath the cockpit with 600 rounds of ammunition. Two Mk 51-14 racks could be mounted to hard points beneath the fuselage, and each of these could carry up to a 2,000-pound store. Additionally, three 14B-1 pylons could be mounted under each wing, with a capacity of 500 pounds per pylon. The maximum total for external stores was 4,000 pounds. The F3H-1N would be armed with the Sidewinder air-to-air missile when it became available.

Less than four months after the initial flight of the first F3H-1N, the first XF3H-1 prototype was lost in an engine related crash in March 1954. Soon thereafter, an F3H-1N was also lost. Throughout the rest of 1954 and early 1955, the F3H-1Ns experienced several engine failures which resulted in groundings that continued to delay the program. Each time the flight testing resumed, there was another crash. In all, there were eight crashes that destroyed six aircraft and killed four pilots. By mid-1955, the Navy had finally had enough, and the production of F3H-1Ns was halted after only fifty-six aircraft had been accepted, including the six that had been lost in accidents. Not only was the engine proving to be completely unreliable, it produced far less than the expected thrust. The magnitude of the J40 engine disaster caused Westinghouse to end its jet engine program shortly thereafter.

In an effort to save the Demon, the Navy ordered a change to the Allison J71-A-2 engine. F3H-1s, BuNos. 133519 and 133521, were fitted with the J71 for evaluation purposes. BuNo. 133519 made its first flight with the J71 in October 1954. The Allison engine provided more power, but it was still considered inadequate for the Demon. It also had some reliability problems, including a tendency to flame out and have compressor stalls, but these were not as severe as those that had been experienced with the J40.

A production version of the Demon with the J71 engine required much more than just the engine change. A number of airframe modifications were necessary. F3H-1N, BuNo. 133520, was converted to the first F3H-2N prototype, and it made its first flight on January 11, 1955. However, it was destroyed in a crash

With an F2H-1 Banshee as a chase plane, the first production F3H-1N lifts off the runway in St. Louis for an early test flight. (McDonnell photograph via the National Naval Aviation Museum)

the following month. BuNo. 133522 was used as the second F3H-2N prototype. The rather significant changes made to the airframe to produce the F3H-2N will be discussed in the next section of this publication. Some of the completed F3H-1Ns were used as trainers for ground personnel or for ground structural testing. Others were scrapped, some without ever making a flight. The proposed F3H-1P photographic reconnaissance version was also abandoned.

The Navy's grounding of the F3H-1N was complete and permanent. Aircraft that were sent to ground training facilities were moved by flatbed cars on trains or by barges. None were permitted to fly to their new locations. The original promise of the Demon to provide the Navy with an advanced aircraft that would equal the Air Force's first Century Series fighters had been destroyed by the failure of the Westinghouse J40 engine. While the Allison J71 would provide the subsequent versions of the aircraft with a measure of success, it fell far short of the potential the Demon could have experienced had it been fitted with an engine that provided sufficient power and reliable performance.

Although no F3H-1Ns remained in the Navy's inventory in 1962 when the standardization of aircraft designations took place, the F-3A designation was assigned to this version of the Demon under the new system.

After a series of engine failures, crashes, and fatalities, the Navy finally canceled the contract for the F3H-1N and ordered that all flying of the aircraft be halted. Completed aircraft were placed on barges and shipped to various facilities for ground testing and training. Most of the F3H-1Ns never made a flight. Here BuNo. 133501 is hoisted off the pier and onto a barge for shipment. (McDonnell photograph via Jim Mesko)

A right rear quarter view of F3H-1N, 133491, shows the long beaver tail fitted to all Demon variants except the F3H-2. The elliptical shaped object under the aircraft is the external starter. This unit could be transported on one of the aircraft's pylons. (Photograph from the collection of the National Naval Aviation Museum)

BuNo. 133489 is seen here in slow speed flight with the leading edge slats and the flaps lowered. Note that the inboard sections on the underside of the horizontal tail surfaces were painted with a heat resistant silver enamel. (McDonnell photograph via the National Naval Aviation Museum)

In addition to being used for the training of ground personnel, a few F3H-1Ns were used for other tests. Here BuNo. 133500 is being used for barrier testing at the Naval Air Test Facility. Interestingly, all of the landing gear doors have been removed for this test. (Official U. S. Navy photograph via the National Naval Aviation Museum)

F3H-1N DATA
(Source: Official U. S. Navy Standard Aircraft Characteristics)

DIMENSIONS
- Wing Area .... 442 sq ft
- Span .... 35 feet, 4 inches
- Mean Aerodynamic Chord .... 155 inches
- Sweepback @ ¼-Chord .... 45 degrees
- Length .... 59 feet, 0 inches
- Height .... 15 feet, 11 inches

WEIGHTS
- Empty .... 18,691 pounds
- Basic .... 19,360 pounds
- Design .... 26,000 pounds
- Combat .... 26,085 pounds
- Maximum Take-Off (Field) .... 34,000 pounds
- Maximum Take-Off (Catapult) .... 30,000 pounds
- Maximum Landing (Field) .... 27,000 pounds
- Maximum Landing (Arrested) .... 23,500 pounds

POWERPLANT
- Number and Model .... (1) J40-WE-22
- Manufacturer .... Westinghouse
- Type .... Axial-Flow
- Length (Including Afterburner) .... 284 inches
- Diameter .... 41 inches
- Augmentation .... Afterburner
- Ratings
  - Afterburner .... 10,900 pounds @ 7,260 RPM
  - Military .... 7,250 pounds @ 7,260 RPM
  - Normal .... 6,500 pounds @ 7,260 RPM

FUEL (JP-4, MIL-F-5624)
Number of Tanks	Total Gallons	Location
3	1,202	Fuselage
4	304	Wing

OIL (Grade 1010, MIL-0-6081) .... 15 Gallons

ELECTRONICS
- UHF Communications AN/ARC-27A
  (With alternate provisions for AN/ARC-1)
- Radar Altimeter AN/APN-22
- UHF Homing AN/ARA-25
- Radio Compass AN/ARN-6
- Radar AN/APG-30
- Radar (Provisions) AN/APQ-50
  (First 30 aircraft only)
- IFF AN/APX-6
- Coder Group AN/APX-89

ORDNANCE
- Guns .... 4 X 20-mm cannon in nose with 600 rounds
- Bombs and Rockets

Racks	Number	Location	Maximum Capacity
MK 51-14	2	Fuselage	2,000 pounds
14B-1	6	Wing	500 pounds

(Maximum stores capacity, 4,000 pounds)

PERFORMANCE (Fighter with full internal fuel)
- Maximum Speed/Altitude .... 506 knots @ 14,000 feet
- Stall Speed, Power Off .... 112.1 knots
- Rate of Climb at Sea Level .... 3,250 feet-per-minute
- Ceiling .... 32,000 feet
- Combat Range .... 980 nautical miles
- Combat Radius .... 345 nautical miles

This F3H-1N was sent to NAS Pensacola to be used for ground training purposes. Note that the inside surfaces, not just the edges, of the landing gear doors on the overall Gloss Sea Blue aircraft were painted solid red. (Official U. S. Navy photograph via the National Naval Aviation Museum)

F3H-2N (F-3C)

Differences between the first production F3H-2N (left) and the previous F3H-1N are evident in this view. Most noticeable is the enlarged wing on the F3H-2N, which was created by extending the root cord aft. The wingspan and the angle of sweepback of the leading edge remained unchanged. Between the production of the F3H-1N and the F3H-2N, the Navy changed from the overall Gloss Sea Blue scheme to Light Gull Gray over white for its fighter aircraft. (McDonnell photograph via Jim Mesko)

The disaster that ended F3H-1N production and almost doomed the entire Demon program was primarily due to the Westinghouse J40 engine rather than the aircraft itself. The design has proven to be a good one with excellent flying and handling qualities. The Navy wanted to continue the program and selected the Allison J71 turbojet as the new engine for the fighter.

The choice of the Allison J71 was not really the one the Navy wanted to make. Of the jet engines entering service in the 1950s, Pratt & Whitney's J57 was clearly the best, offering excellent power and high reliability. Because of this, it was in great demand. The Air Force was using eight for each of its B-52 bombers and four for each of its C-135 Stratolifters and KC-135 Stratotankers. In different versions, both with and without afterburners, it was being produced for the F-100 Super Sabre, F-101 Voodoo, and F-102 Delta Dagger, as well as the B-57 Canberra and even the Lockheed U-2 Dragon Lady. The SM-62 Snark missile also used the J-57, and the civilian market was adding to the demand for Pratt & Whitney's J57 for the Boeing 707 and 720, as well as the Douglas DC-8 airliners. More than sixty years after its introduction, the J57 is still in use by both military and civilian aviation as this is written.

The Navy had also acquired J57s for some of its aircraft, including the A3D Skywarrior. When the Westinghouse J40 proved to be a failure, it affected the F3H Demon and F4D-1 Skyray fight-

BuNo. 133549 was the first production F3H-2N, and it was fitted with an instrumentation probe for test flights. This view shows the pitot probe in the original position under the nose. It would later be moved to the base of the windscreen when antennas were mounted in the lower nose section. Also visible in this photograph is the original one-piece windscreen as used on the previous F3H-1N. It would soon be replaced with a framed three-piece design. (McDonnell photo via the National Naval Aviation Museum)

Above and below: BuNo. 133550 was the second production F3H-2N. These two photographs provide a study of the early features of the F3H-2N including the pitot probe under the nose and the one-piece windscreen. Also note the lack of spoilers on top of the wings. These photos were taken before the wing warping problem was discovered. Further, the F3H-2N originally did not have the boundary layer fence on each wing, however these were soon added after flight testing proved they provided advantages in controlling boundary layer air over the swept wing surfaces. (Top, McDonnell photograph via the National Naval Aviation Museum; bottom, McDonnell photograph from the collection of Don Spering)

Two F3H-1Ns, BuNos. 133520 and 133522, were modified to serve as F3H-2N prototypes. They retained their overall Gloss Sea Blue paint schemes even after the conversion. BuNo. 133520 crashed in February 1955, but 133522 continued to be used as a test aircraft for quite some time. It is shown here serving as a tanker during the development of the in-flight refueling package for the Demon. (Photograph from the collection of Don Spering)

ers, both of which were originally designed to use the troubled powerplant. The Navy was able to acquire enough J57s to replace the J40 in the Skyray and the few subsequent F5D Skylancers, but another replacement had to be found for the Demon. It should also be noted that the later and highly successful Navy jet fighter, Chance Vought's F-8 Crusader, would be powered by the Pratt & Whitney J57.

To replace the J40 in the Demon, the Navy really had little choice other than the Allison J71. While being a far less desirable powerplant than the J57, it was simply the best alternative available. The Navy had originally specified that the J71 be used in the A3D Skywarrior, and it was installed in the two XA3D-1 prototypes. But the engine proved to be unsatisfactory, and the J57 was selected to replace it on the YA3D-1 and all subsequent production versions of the Skywarrior. Interestingly, the A3D's half-brother in the U. S. Air Force, the B-66 Destroyer, was equipped with Allison J71s throughout its service life, and it was the only production aircraft other than the Demon to use the J71. So as the change was made from the Westinghouse J40 to the Allison J71 for the Demon, the Navy knew the choice was less than optimum, because of its experience with the J71 in the XA3D-1 prototypes. Nevertheless, and in spite of its problems, the Allison J71 was far superior to the Westinghouse J40 it replaced, and it offered a significant increase in power and performance for the Demon. This improvement can be studied by comparing the performance figures for the F3H-2N at the end of this section with the corresponding figures for the F3H-1N.

In 1955, two F3H-1Ns, BuNos. 133519 and 133521, were fitted with the J71 and used as test aircraft. Even before test flights were made with these two aircraft, it was apparent that the Demon would have to undergo considerable redesign before it could become operational with the new engine.

The most noticeable of the design changes was an increase in wing area which was required due to the greater weight of the aircraft with the J71 engine. This was accomplished by increasing the wing cord at the root so that the trailing edge was further aft than on the F3H-1N. The wing area for the F3H-2N and subsequent versions of the Demon was 519 square feet with a mean aerodynamic chord of 186.70 inches compared to a wing area of 442 square feet and a MAC of 155 inches for the F3H-1N.

Two F3H-2N prototypes, BuNos. 133520 and 133522, were ordered, and these were constructed using two F3H-1N airframes. The improved performance over the F3H-1N was substantial, but BuNo. 133520 was lost in a crash in February 1955. Its loss was thought to have been caused by a failure of the one-piece windscreen. This incident resulted in the one-piece windscreen being replaced by a three-piece framed design early in the production run of F3H-2Ns, and all aircraft completed with the early windscreens were retrofitted.

Early production F3H-2Ns had their pitot probe located under the forward fuselage where it had been on the F3H-1N. However, during the production of F3H-2Ns, the probe was moved to the base of the windscreen when antennas were located in the lower nose section. Later, a static pressure boom was added to the right wing near the tip.

An F3H-2N from the "Tomcatters" of VF-31 flies past NAS Mayport, Florida. In the background are the aircraft carriers USS SHANGRI-LA, CVA-38, (left) and USS FRANKLIN D. ROOSEVELT, CVA-42. The two large pylons under the fuselage and the three smaller ones under the right wing are visible in this banked view. By the time this photograph was taken, the pitot probe had been moved from its original position under the nose to the base of the windscreen. (National Naval Aviation Museum)

Another change had to do with a problem that surfaced shortly after the F3H-2N entered operational service. During high-speed rolls, the wings would warp. Rather than redesign the wing, strengthening its structure, spoilers were added on top of each wing to spread out the forces caused by the high-speed aileron rolls. This solved the problem, and the spoilers became standard on all subsequent Demon production aircraft as well as being retrofitted to earlier airframes.

Jet engines in the 1950s were not very fuel efficient, and the addition of afterburners for fighter aircraft made fuel consumption an even greater problem. This led to the development of aerial tankers and in-flight refueling systems that would become standard for all future fighter development. But the Demon had been designed without an in-flight refueling probe, so a detachable probe was developed. Designed to work with the Navy's probe and drogue system, it could be installed on the upper surface of the right air inlet. Once it became operational, Demons usually had the probe installed, particularly when deployed aboard aircraft carriers. While this improved the Demon's endurance and range capabilities, pilots complained that the extra weight of the probe degraded the aircraft's performance that was already limited by a less than adequate engine.

A problem that surfaced early with the Demon and its J71 engine was that the engine's casing would contract and come in contact with the turbine blades in the cold damp temperatures at high altitudes. This would cause a flameout or even engine failure. To eliminate the problem, Allison shaved off the turbine blades enough so that the casing had room to contract without coming in contact with them, but this caused a dramatic loss in power. Performance that could previously be attained at 30,000 feet could now only be reached at 20,000 feet.

As originally produced, all F3H-2Ns were fitted with an ejection seat designed by McDonnell. After several fatalities occurred when this seat failed to function properly, the Navy changed to a different seat designed by Martin Baker. Once available, these were retrofitted to all F3H-2Ns still in service.

The F3H-2N was armed with four 20-mm cannons in the lower nose section with 720 rounds of ammunition distributed between the four guns. This was an increase of 120 rounds over the 600 rounds carried in the F3H-1N. A Mk-16, Mod 9 Automatic Fire Control System provided for the accurate employment of the weapons, and an AN-N-6A gun camera recorded the results of any engagement. Additional weapons could be carried on six under-wing stations and two fuselage stations. In fact, the Demon was certified to deliver a variety of bombs and other air-to-ground weapons as shown in the external stores chart on page 59 of this publication. This gave the aircraft a fighter-bomber capability, although these weapons, other than small practice bombs, were seldom carried operationally.

The Demon was designed to employ the AAM-N-7A (later AIM-9B) Sidewinder infrared-homing air-to-air missile when it became available. The Sidewinders could be carried on stations 1, 3, 6, and 8, and an Aero 1A launch rail had to be fitted to the pylon to carry the missile. While the F3H-2N could carry four Sidewinders, photographs indicate that no more than two were usually loaded.

To supplement the air-to-air capability of the four 20-mm cannons, rocket pods carrying 2.75-inch rockets could be carried on the wing pylons. These were attached directly to the under-wing pylons. The F3H-2N could not employ the Sparrow I or Sparrow III missile, because its AN/APG-51A radar was not capable of guiding them, so the Sidewinder was the only guided air-to-air missile used with this version of the Demon as originally delivered.

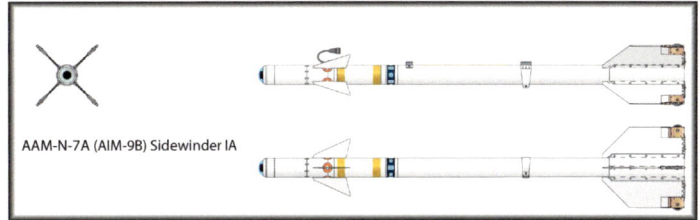

When the AAM-N-7A (later AIM-9B) Sidewinder air-to-air missile became operational, up to four could be carried by the F3H-2N with its AN/APG-51A radar. That radar was not capable of guiding either version of the Sparrow missile, so the Sidewinder, which was not dependent on a radar for guidance, was the only guided air-to-air missile the F3H-2N could employ as built. However, some F3H-2Ns were subsequently upgraded to F3H-2 standards with AN/APQ-51B radars that could guide the Sparrow III missile. This drawing shows the correct configuration and markings for a live AAM-N-7A or AIM-9B. Note that this version of the Sidewinder did not have the brown band that appeared on later versions of the heat-seeking missile indicating the presence of a live rocket motor. (Copyright drawing by Jim Rotramel)

The two fuselage stations could each carry a 282-gallon fuel tank, but the drag caused by the two tanks more than offset the advantages of the extra fuel and thus reduced the aircraft's range as well as performance. By carrying only one tank, the increase in range was reportedly only five miles over internal fuel alone, so the tanks were seldom carried operationally.

The F3H-2N became operational in March 1956 with VF-14, and that unit made its first deployment in Demons aboard USS FORRESTAL, CVA-59, in 1957. Over the next two years, more fighter squadrons transitioned to the F3H-2N and began making deployments with both the Atlantic and Pacific Fleets.

During their operational service, some F3H-2Ns were upgraded to F3H-2 standards by changing the radar from the

VF-14 became the first squadron to make a deployment with the Demon when the "Top Hatters" sailed to the Mediterranean aboard the new supercarrier, USS FORRESTAL, CVA-59, in 1957. Note the lack of spoilers on the wings and the fact that there is no static pressure boom on the right wing tip of these early F3H-2Ns. At the time this photo was taken, the detachable in-flight refueling probe had not entered service with Demon squadrons. (National Naval Aviation Museum)

AN/APG-51A to the AN/APQ-51B. This improvement added the capability to employ the Sparrow III semi-active homing missile, significantly increasing the all-weather capability of the aircraft. Prior to gaining the Sparrow III capability, the F3H-2N could use only its 20-mm cannons or rocket pods in bad weather, because the Sidewinder required a clear air environment for its IR seeker to lock onto a target. Once upgraded to F3H-2 standards, Demons originally produced as F3H-2Ns were seen serving in squadrons alongside production F3H-2s.

Under the standardization of aircraft designations directed by the Department of Defense in September 1962, the F3H-2N was redesignated the F-3C. BuNos. 133520 and 133522, which had served as the two F3H-2N prototypes, were given the YF-3C designation, although they no longer existed.

A few Demons were used to test new systems and equipment. In this photo, F3H-2N, BuNo. 133581, is shown serving as a launch aircraft for a Beechcraft AQM-37A supersonic target drone. The drone is being carried on a special pylon attached to station 3. (Beechcraft photograph from the collection of Don Spering)

This close-up shows an AQM-37A supersonic target drone being loaded on the F3H-2N. (Beechcraft photograph from the collection of Don Spering)

Left two photos: VF-114's markings are displayed in these photos of F3H-2N, BuNo. 136973. They consist of a red fuselage flash and a red fin cap, outlined in black. The tips of the wings are also painted red. VF-114 is painted high on the aft fuselage. Note the modex which begins with a 4, unusual for Demons, with most squadrons having a nose number starting with a 1 or a 2. LT. D. E. WAYHAM is stenciled just above the modex. (Both, National Naval Aviation Museum)

A left rear view of F3H-2N, BuNo. 133610, provides a good look at the markings used on VF-124's Demons. Also note the white area painted on the aft fuselage below the vertical tail that indicates the travel limits of the stabilator. (National Naval Aviation Museum)

F3H-2N DATA
(Source: Official U. S. Navy Standard Aircraft Characteristics)

DIMENSIONS
Wing Area..519 square feet
   Span..35 feet, 4 inches
   Mean Aerodynamic Chord...........................15 feet, 6 inches
   Sweepback @ ¼-Chord....................43 degrees, 12 minutes
   Length..59 feet, 0 inches
   Height...14 feet, 7 inches

WEIGHTS
   Empty..20,645 pounds
   Basic...21,542 pounds
   Design...26,000 pounds
   Combat...28,050 pounds
   Maximum Take-Off (Field)...........................35,378 pounds
   Maximum Landing (Field)............................29,000 pounds

POWERPLANT
   Number and Model...(1) J71-A-2
   Manufacturer..Allison
   Type...Axial-Flow
   Length (Including Afterburner)............................287 inches
   Diameter...43 inches
   Augmentation...Afterburner
   Ratings
     Afterburner.........................14,500 pounds @ 6,100 RPM
     Military..............................10,200 pounds @ 6,100 RPM
     Normal................................8,800 pounds @ 6,100 RPM

FUEL (JP-4, MIL-F-5624)
Number of Tanks	Total Gallons	Location
3	1,200	Fuselage
4	306	Wing
2	282 (each)	External

OIL (Grade 1010, MIL-0-6081).....................Integral With Engine

ELECTRONICS
   UHF Communications.....................................AN/ARC-27A
   UHF Direction Finding....................................AN/ARA-25
   Low Frequency ADF..AN/ARN-6
   Radar Altimeter...AN/APN-22
   Radar...AN/APG-51A
   IFF..AN/APX-6/6B
   Coder Group...AN/APX-89
   Special Equipment................Provisions for ADF, AN/ARN-21
                    as an alternate for AN/ARN-6

ORDNANCE
   Guns................4 X 20-mm cannon in nose with 720 rounds
   Bombs and Rockets

Racks	Number	Location	Maximum Capacity
MK 51-14	2	Fuselage	2,000 pounds
Aero 14 or 15	6	Wing	500 pounds

     (Maximum stores capacity, 4,000 pounds)

PERFORMANCE (Clean with full internal fuel)
   Maximum Speed/Altitude...................580 knots @ sea level
   Stall Speed, Power Off.......................................109.5 knots
   Rate of Climb at Sea Level..................5,500 feet-per-minute
   Ceiling...39,000 feet
   Combat Range.......................................1,040 nautical miles
   Combat Radius..365 nautical miles

The first markings used by VF-151 on its Demons are seen in this photograph of F3H-2N, BuNo. 133594, and F3H-2, BuNo. 146734. The only unit marking is the VF-151 painted high on the aft fuselage. The NL tail code is in a vertical block style of lettering. Note that the upper two 20-mm cannons have been removed from each aircraft and their gun ports are covered over. Each Demon carries a single under-wing pylon with an AERO 1A launcher for the Sidewinder missile. (National Naval Aviation Museum)

Two of VF-141s F3H-2Ns fly in formation in February 1961. Note that the gun armament on these Demons has been reduced to only the two lower cannons. Launch rails for Sparrow III missiles are on the outboard pylons, and rails for Sidewinders are on the inboard wing pylons. (National Naval Aviation Museum)

Right: Two of VF-193's Demons fly past USS BONHOMME RICHARD. The aircraft in the foreground is F3H-2N, BuNo. 133593. It has been upgraded to F3H-2 standards to employ the Sparrow III missile, and one of the missiles can be seen on the outboard pylon. Note that this Demon retains it original long beaver tail. (National Naval Aviation Museum)

F3H-2M (MF-3B)

F3H-2M, BuNo. 133629, was used in the AAM-N-2 Sparrow I test program at NAS Point Mugu. It is shown here with four developmental versions of the missile on its wing stations. The pointed nose of the Sparrow I is evident in this photograph. (National Naval Aviation Museum)

Bureau Number 133569 served as the prototype for the F3H-2M version of the Demon and it was followed into production by seventy-nine additional examples of this variant. Of the three versions of the Demon that became operational with Navy fleet squadrons, the F3H-2M was the least successful and remained in service for the shortest period of time. This was due to two factors. First, the primary missile armament intended for use with the F3H-2M, the AAM-N-2 (later AIM-7A) Sparrow I missile, was a failure. Second, the AN/APQ-51A radar installed in the F3H-2M did not provide position data on the target. Accordingly, there was no radar scope in the cockpit. The radar simply provided ranging information to the target which had to be acquired visually by the pilot. This meant that the F3H-2M was not an all-weather or night fighter. It was limited to clear air engagements, and pilots who flew it referred to it as the "day fighter" version of the Demon.

The fact that the F3H-2M was not an all-weather interceptor seems odd, given that the Navy had specified that the aircraft fulfill the all-weather/night interceptor role before the first F3H-1N was even built. Adding to the mystery is the fact that radar guided missiles were developed specifically to arm all-weather fighters. They were necessary, because infrared guided missiles like the Sidewinder and some versions of the Falcon could only be used in a clear air environment. Radar guided missiles were supposed to be able to engage targets in any kind of weather. Yet even with its intended Sparrow I armament, the radar used in the F3H-2M limited its use to the day fighter role.

The F3H-2M was developed and produced concurrently with, and joined the fleet shortly after, the F3H-2N. But by the time it became operational, the unreliability of the Sparrow I had become known, and the limitations of the AN/APQ-51A radar would mean that the F3H-2M would only be assigned to three squadrons, one of which would never make a deployment. The eighty F3H-2Ms, which included the prototype, saw a very short operational life before being withdrawn from service by early 1959.

To comprehend the lack of success that plagued the Sparrow I, it is necessary to understand how its guidance system worked along with its severe limitations. The missile was called a beam rider, because the radar in the launching aircraft generated a beam that was pointed at the intended target. When launched, the missile rode the beam to the target, in theory. In practice, however, if the missile veered off course enough for its antenna to lose contact with the narrow beam pointing to the target, guidance would be lost, and the missile would go ballistic. Further, the pilot had to visually see the target and hold the narrow beam on the target by keeping it centered in his gun sight. This meant that the system was only effective in clear air against a target flying straight and level. If the target was maneuvering, an attempt by the attacking pilot to keep the radar beam on the target could pull the beam away from the missile, and it would go ballistic. Thus the beam-riding guidance system was impractical in an actual combat environment. The antenna on the missile that received the radar beam was located at the aft end rather than in the front, and this resulted in the Sparrow I having a much more pointed nose than

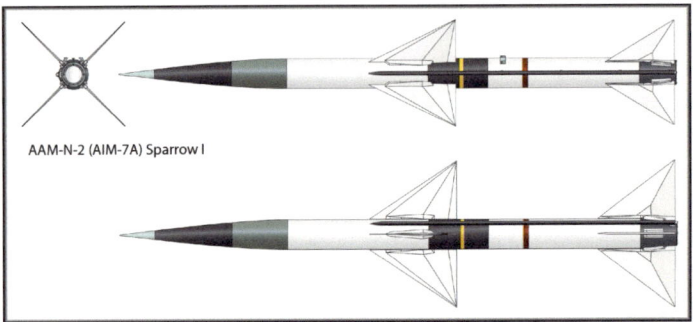

These drawings show what an operational Sparrow I missile looked like. The yellow band indicates the presence of a live warhead, and the brown band signifies that the missile has a rocket motor installed. (Copyright drawing by Jim Rotramel)

VF-61 was the only fleet squadron to operate the F3H-2M version of the Demon on the Atlantic coast. Note the blue Sparrow I AERO 3A launch rails on the Light Gull Gray over white aircraft. This was a fairly common sight for both Sparrow I AERO 3A and Sparrow III AERO 4A launch rails. (National Naval Aviation Museum)

When the F3H-2Ms were withdrawn from service in 1959, some of the airframes were used for ground training. This photograph shows an F3H-2M at the Naval Air Technical Training Unit at Lakehurst, New Jersey, being used to train airframe repair and maintenance personnel. The Demon was painted Sea Blue. Shortly after this photo was taken in 1968, the hulks of the Demons were burned in exercises to train fire-fighting personnel. (Spering)

subsequent radar guided missiles which had a radome covering a radar antenna at the forward end.

The lack of reliability was another problem with the Sparrow I. As Len Kaine points out in the chapter, Demon Daze, four pilots from VF-61 were selected to test fire Sparrow Is at a weapons firing area when that squadron was equipped with F3H-2M Demons. Each of the four aircraft took their turn engaging the target, and not one of the Sparrow Is even came off the launch rail. The four F3H-2Ms returned to their base with the missiles still under their left wings.

Up to four Sparrow I missiles could be loaded on the F3H-2M. Mounting the missile required that an Aero 3A launch rail be attached to the pylon, and the missile was then mounted on the launch rails. Interestingly, most Aero 3A launch rails were manufactured when the overall Gloss Sea Blue scheme was specified for fighters, so it was not unusual to see blue launch rails on the Light Gull Gray over white Demons.

The Sparrow I was heavier than the Sidewinder, more expensive, and far more complex. Since it could only be used in a clear air environment like the Sidewinder, the latter was more practical, reliable, and cost effective. The Sidewinder was also a launch-and-leave missile, meaning that as soon as it was launched, the pilot could maneuver his aircraft as the tactical situation dictated, because there was no necessity to keep a radar beam held on the target. As a result, the Sparrow I was short lived, and no more than 2,000 were ever produced. However, the semi-active homing version, the Sparrow III, was much more successful and could be used on the F3H-2 and F3H-2Ns that were upgraded to F3H-2M standards. More than 25,000 examples of this version of the Sparrow would be produced, and it would then be followed by many thousands more units of later Sparrow versions. It would remain the U. S. military's primary radar guided missile for more than four decades.

Contrary to what has been reported in other publications, the F3H-2M could not employ the Sparrow III missile, and no upgrade was ever done to this version of the Demon that would have made this possible as was the case with the F3H-2N. As a result, F3H-2Ms were armed with the Sidewinder missile when it became operational, and rocket pods carrying 2.75-inch rockets supplemented the air-to-air armament.

The only Atlantic Fleet squadron to operate the F3H-2M was VF-61. The Jolly Rogers began their transition to the Demon in September 1956. Although they flew qualifications aboard USS FRANKLIN D. ROOSEVELT, CVA-42, and USS SARATOGA, CVA-60, they never made a full overseas deployment. After the F3H-2M fell out of favor with the Navy, VF-61 was decommissioned in April 1959, although other Navy fighter squadrons flying the F3H-2N and F3H-2 variants remained operational with the Demon for as long as five more years.

VF-24 was one of only two Pacific Fleet squadrons to become operational in the F3H-2M. The "Corsairs" began to receive their Demons in mid-1957, and after a year of qualifications and training, they made a deployment aboard USS LEXINGTON, CVA-16, from July to December 1958. By the time they returned from the cruise, the Navy had decided the F3H-2M had to go, so VF-24 immediately began a transition to the Grumman F11F-1 Tiger.

The other Pacific Fleet squadron to fly the F3H-2M version of the Demon was VF-112 which began its transition to the F3H-2M in late 1956. Following training and a number of carrier qualification periods aboard several carriers, VF-112 made one deployment aboard USS TICONDEROGA, CVA-14, that lasted from August 1958 until February 1959. Upon the completion of this one cruise with the Demon, they began transitioning to the Douglas A4D Skyhawk, and the squadron's designation was changed to VA-112.

A review of the F3H-2M's service reveals that this Demon variant was completely withdrawn from operational service during the first half of 1959. Only three squadrons flew it, and only two

One of two Pacific Fleet squadrons to fly the F3H-2M was VF-24. The "Corsairs" made only one deployment with the Demon before transitioning to the F11F-1 Tiger immediately upon the completion of that cruise in December 1958. (National Naval Aviation Museum)

deployments were ever made. By comparison, the more capable F3H-2N and F2H-2 served twice as long in twenty-one different fleet squadrons. The F3H-2M was also produced in the far fewer numbers than either of these two other versions. Although completely withdrawn from service by mid-1959, three years before the Department of Defense ordered a standardization of military aircraft designations in September 1962, F3H-2Ms were redesignated MF-3Bs. Bureau Number 133569, which had served as the F3H-2M prototype, was redesignated YMF-3B.

F3H-2M DATA
(Source: Official U. S. Navy Standard Aircraft Characteristics)

DIMENSIONS
Wing
- Area..519 square feet
- Span..35 feet, 4 inches
- Mean Aerodynamic Chord........................15 feet, 6 inches
- Sweepback @ ¼-Chord...................43 degrees, 12 minutes
- Length..59 feet, 0 inches
- Height..14 feet, 7 inches

WEIGHTS
- Empty...20,322 pounds
- Basic..20,979 pounds
- Design..26,000 pounds
- Combat...27,859 pounds
- Maximum Take-Off (Field)..........................33,112 pounds
- Maximum Take-Off (Catapult)......................30,000 pounds
- Maximum Landing (Field)...........................24,823 pounds
- Maximum Landing (Arrested).......................23,500 pounds

POWERPLANT
- Number and Model..J71-A-2
- Manufacturer..Allison
- Type..Axial-Flow
- Length (Including Afterburner).............................287 inches
- Diameter..43 inches
- Augmentation..Afterburner
- Ratings
  - Afterburner...................14,500 pounds @ 6,100 RPM
  - Military...........................10,200 pounds @ 6,100 RPM
  - Normal............................8,800 pounds @ 6,100 RPM

FUEL (JP-4, MIL-F-5624)
Number of Tanks	Total Gallons	Location
3	1,200	Fuselage
4	306	Wing
2	282 (each)	External

OIL (Grade 1010, MIL-0-7808).................Integral With Engine

ELECTRONICS
- UHF Communications.............................AN/ARC-27A
- UHF Direction Finding..............................AN/ARA-25
- Low Frequency ADF.................................AN/ARN-6
- Radar Altimeter....................................... AN/APN-22
- Radar..AN/APG-51A
- IFF...AN/APX-6/6B
- Coder Group......................................AN/APX-89
- Special Equipment........Provisions for ADF, AN/ARN-21
  as an alternate for AN/ARN-6

ORDNANCE
- Guns................4 X 20-mm cannon in nose with 720 rounds
- Fire Control.....................................ACS AERO 10
- Bombs and Rockets

Racks	Number	Location	Maximum Capacity
MK 51-13	2	Fuselage	2,000 pounds
Aero 15A	6	Wing	500 pounds

(Maximum stores capacity, 4,000 pounds)

PERFORMANCE (With Two Sparrow I Missiles)
- Maximum Speed/Altitude................530 knots @ 10,000 feet
- Stall Speed, Power Off......................................110.2 knots
- Rate of Climb at Sea Level...................4,950 feet-per-minute
- Ceiling..36,400 feet
- Combat Range...996 nautical miles
- Combat Radius...422 nautical miles

VF-112 was the other Pacific Fleet squadron to become operational with the F3H-2M. As with VF-24, the unit made only one deployment with the Demon, after which it transitioned to the A4D Skyhawk in early 1959. One of VF-112's F3H-2Ms is shown here on Cat TWO aboard USS TICONDEROGA, CVA-14, during that cruise. Note the blue AERO 3A launcher for the Sparrow I missile on the outboard wing pylon and the white AERO 1A launcher for the Sidewinder missile on the inboard pylon. (National Naval Aviation Museum)

F3H-2 (F-3B)

The plane captain helps the pilot of an F3H-2 from VF-141 strap into the cockpit prior to a mission aboard USS LEXINGTON, CVA-16, in October 1961. The Demon is armed with two AAM-N-6 (AIM-7C) Sparrow III missiles mounted on stations 1 and 8. In this view, the light tan colored radome of the Sparrow III is visible, and it is evident that the forward end of the missile is not as pointed as on the Sparrow I. (National Naval Aviation Museum)

The final and definitive Demon Variant was the F3H-2. It entered production and service approximately a year after the F3H-2N and F3H-2M, and it was built in far larger numbers than the two previous variants with 239 being delivered. This compared to 142 F3H-2Ns (including the two prototypes) and eighty F3H-2Ms. The first flight of a production F3H-2 took place in July 1957, and squadrons began to transition to the F3H-2 in September of that year. There were two ways to distinguish an F3H-2 from the two earlier Demon versions. First, the Bureau Number of all F3H-2s began with 14, while those assigned to the F3H-2N and F3H-2M began with 13. Second, the beaver tail at the aft end of the fuselage was shorter on the F3H-2, and it had a rounded top rather than a flat one.

The F3H-2 had a slightly different version of the Allison J71 engine than the F3H-2N and F3H-2M. While the two earlier variants used the J71-A-2, the F3H-2 was fitted with the J71-A-2B. It was just under an inch smaller in diameter than the J71-A-2, and it did not produce quite as much thrust. But it was intended to correct some of the reliability problems experienced with the earlier powerplant. Thrust figures for the engines can be found in the data charts that follow the text for each Demon variant.

With the F3H-2, the Navy finally had the missile-armed, all-weather interceptor it had always expected the Demon to be. The F3H-2M had been limited essentially to the day fighter role, because with its AN/APQ-51A radar, it could not find its targets at night or in bad weather conditions. This required the pilot to acquire the target visually. The F3H-2N, with its AN/APG-51A radar, could locate targets at night and in bad weather conditions, but it was limited to attacking with its 20-mm cannons and 2.75-inch

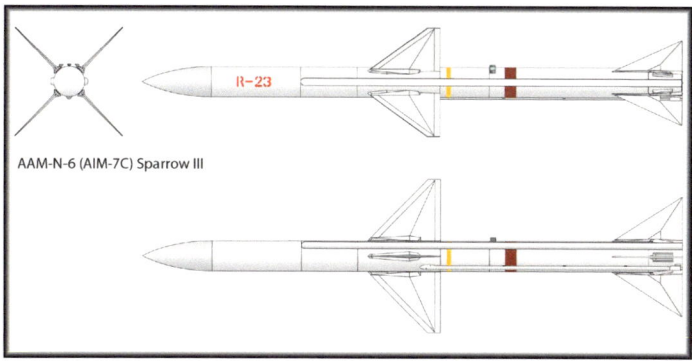

These drawings show the design of the AAM-N-6 (AIM-7C) Sparrow III missile that provided the Demon, and later other jet fighters, with a true all-weather air-to-air guided missile capability. Compare the design of this missile with that of the Sparrow I illustrated in the F3H-2M section of this chapter. The general design of the Sparrow III would remain basically unchanged for the later versions of the weapon that would continue to arm U. S. fighters past the turn of the century, with only detail changes being made. (Copyright drawing by Jim Rotramel)

An F3H-2 in the markings of VF-131 is shown in May 1962, just a few months prior to the designation change to F-3B. F3H-2 is stenciled just above the small bureau number on the fuselage above the exhaust nozzle. From this angle, the shorter beaver tail with the rounded top is clearly visible. This was a distinguishing feature of the F3H-2 variant. (National Naval Aviation Museum)

rockets carried in pods when it was operating in cloudy conditions, because the Sidewinder could not be used in cloudy or bad weather. It was the F3H-2 version that finally brought it all together with its AN/APQ-51B radar which had the added capability of guiding the semi-active homing AAM-N-6 (later AIM-7C) Sparrow III air-to-air missile. Finally, the Demon could not only find a target in any weather, it could engage at greater distances with a reliable radar guided missile.

The semi-active homing guidance used in the Sparrow III, which made it far more successful than the earlier Sparrow I, was a complete rethinking of how radar guided missiles should work. The beam-riding Sparrow I was designed to ride a narrow beam generated by the launching aircraft and continually pointed at the target. The missile actually "saw" the beam with an antenna in its tail that looked to the rear at the radar that was generating the beam rather than forward toward the target. The semi-active homing guidance system used in the Sparrow III was quite different. The radar in the launching aircraft illuminated the target with radar energy. Rather than being a narrow beam, the energy transmitted from the radar fanned out in a conical pattern from the antenna, covering a large area in front of the aircraft. As long as the target was inside the cone, it reflected energy back to the radar unit to provide position information on the scope in the cockpit as well as to the antenna in the forward end of the missile. The target could be designated to the missile, which would then lock on to the reflected energy and follow it to the intercept. This system did require the launching aircraft to continually illuminate the target with the radar energy until the missile destroyed it, but because the radar energy was in the shape of a large cone, rather than a narrow beam, it was far easier to keep a maneuvering target within the cone until the missile completed the intercept. The semi-active homing system proved to be far more reliable and successful than the beam-rider system, and it became the standard for all subsequent radar guided air-to-air missiles as well as many surface-to-air missiles like the U. S. Army's Hawk and the Navy's Sea Sparrow.

Up to four Sparrow IIIs could be loaded on stations 1, 3, 6 and 8 using AERO 4A launchers, but typically, only two Sparrow IIIs were carried. To cover any scenario that may be encountered, F3H-2s would often be armed with two Sparrow III missiles and two Sidewinders. When this load was carried, photographic evidence indicates that the two Sparrow IIIs were usually loaded on stations 1 and 8, and the two Sidewinders were inboard on stations 3 and 6. However, in a few photos, this loading is reversed.

As the Navy began to rely more and more on guided missiles for its interceptors, the upper two 20-mm cannons in F3H-2s were often deleted and their gun ports covered over to reduce the weight of the aircraft. In some cases, all four guns were removed, leaving the F3H-2 armed only with guided missiles. The thinking in the late 1950s was that guns were obsolete and that guided missiles would destroy enemy aircraft at far greater ranges than guns could be employed. It was this thinking that led to the Demon's replacement, the F-4 Phantom, being designed without any internal gun system. Such thinking would later prove to be a big mistake during the Phantom's aerial engagements over Vietnam, and subsequent Navy fighters were designed with internal cannon armament.

It should be noted that it has been reported elsewhere that the F3H-2N had six under-wing pylons, compared to four in the previous Demon variants. The fact is that all production versions of the Demon, including the ill-fated F3H-1N, could be fitted with six pylons under the wings. Two additional pylons could be installed under the fuselage.

During production of the F3H-2, the Navy specified that the Demon be fitted with a Martin Baker H5 ejection seat, and this change was made on the production line starting with BuNo. 146709. As this was happening, the Martin Baker seat was also being retrofitted to the earlier versions of the Demon to replace the original problematic McDonnell ejection seat. Artwork illustrating both ejection seats used in the Demon can be found in the Demon Details chapter of this publication.

It was a relatively simple matter to upgrade the AN/APG-51A radar in existing F3H-2Ns to the AN/APQ-51B, as used in the F3H-2. This was rather quickly accomplished, thus adding the capability to employ the Sparrow III missile to the F3H-2N. Once upgraded to F3H-2 standards, the F3H-2Ns served alongside the F3H-2s in Demon squadrons. Contrary to what has been reported in another publication, the upgrade did not include changing the original longer beaver tail of the F3H-2N to the shorter one fitted to the F3H-2. While this may have happened in some cases when repairs to the airframe were necessary, photographic evidence clearly shows upgraded F3H-2Ns with Sparrow III missiles flying with F3H-2s, and the F3H-2Ns still have their original long beaver tails.

By early-1959, all F3H-2Ms had been withdrawn from fleet squadrons, and by 1960, F3H-2Ns had been upgraded to F3H-2 standards. For the remainder of the Demon's operational service, they served in as many as twenty Navy fighter squadrons providing all-weather air defense for the fleet. Until replaced by the F-4 Phantom, they were the only shipboard fighters capable of employing the Sparrow III, radar guided missile.

In 1962, the F3H-2 was redesignated the F-3B under the standardization of military aircraft designations directed by the Department of Defense. In its final years of operational service many Demons had a red beacon added to the top of the vertical tail.

F3H-2 DATA
(Source: Official U. S. Navy Standard Aircraft Characteristics)

DIMENSIONS
Wing
- Area..519 square feet
- Span..35 feet, 4 inches
- Mean Aerodynamic Chord......................15 feet, 6 inches
- Sweepback @ ¼-Chord...................43 degrees, 12 minutes
- Length..58 feet, 11.5 inches
- Height..14 feet, 6.6 inches

WEIGHTS
- Empty..21,287 pounds
- Basic..22,293 pounds
- Design..26,000 pounds
- Combat..31,145 pounds
- Maximum Take-Off (Field)......................39,000 pounds
- Maximum Landing (Arrested)..................26,700 pounds

POWERPLANT
- Number and Model..............................(1) J71-A-2B
- Manufacturer..Allison
- Type..Axial-Flow
- Length (Including Afterburner)..............287.1 inches
- Diameter..42.1 inches
- Augmentation..Afterburner
- Ratings
  - Afterburner....................14,400 pounds @ 6,175 RPM
  - Military............................10,000 pounds @ 6,175 RPM
  - Normal..............................8,700 pounds @ 6,000 RPM

FUEL (JP-4, MIL-F-5624)

Number of Tanks	Total Gallons	Location
3	1,200	Fuselage
4	306	Wing
2	282 (each)	External

OIL (Grade 1010, MIL-1-7808)..................Integral With Engine

ELECTRONICS
- UHF Communications..............................AN/ARC-27A
- UHF Direction Finding..............................AN/ARA-25
- Short Range Navigation (ADF)....................AN/ARN-21
- Radar Altimeter.......................................AN/APN-22
- Radar..AN/APG-51B
- IFF..AN/APX-6/6B
- Coder Group...AN/APX-89
- Missile Guidance Set...............................AN/APA-127
- Missile Launching Set...............................AN/ASA-23

ORDNANCE
- Guns................4 X 20-mm cannon in nose with 760 rounds
- Gun Camera...AN-N-6A
- Bombs and Rockets

Racks	Number	Location	Maximum Capacity
MK 51-13	2	Fuselage	2,000 pounds
Aero 15A	6	Wing	500 pounds

(Maximum stores capacity, 4,000 pounds)

PERFORMANCE (With Two Sparrow III Missiles)
- Maximum Speed/Altitude................Mach .88 @ 25,000 feet
- Stall Speed, Power Off..................................116 knots
- Rate of Climb at Sea Level...................4,840 feet-per-minute
- Ceiling...34,000 feet
- Combat Range...985 nautical miles
- Combat Radius..336 nautical miles

Below: The various antenna locations found on the F3H-2 are indicated on this photograph of the F3H-2 prototype. Most of the antennas shown here were also the same as used on the F3H-2N and F3H-2M. (McDonnell)

F3H DEMON PILOTS' REPORT 'DEMON DAZE'

Len "Ski" Kaine is a retired Naval Aviator who flew several jet fighters including the Demon and Crusader. He is now president of the Golden Rule Society, a charity he founded that is dedicated to making a better world. (Photo courtesy of Len Kaine)

Author's Note: As work on this publication was beginning, I was put in contact with Captain Len Kaine, USN (Ret.), who flew several types of fighters in the Navy including the F3H-2M Demon as a pilot with the "Jolly Rogers" of VF-61. Len later flew more than one hundred combat missions in Vietnam, and his Navy career included flying no less than fourteen different types of aircraft. After retirement from the Navy, Len flew seven different types of aircraft with U.S. Airways, retiring as an airline captain in 1996.

In 1972, Len founded the Golden Rule Society, a charitable organization dedicated to making this a better world. He remains as president of the Golden Rule Society to this day. His charitable work has brought him many awards, including a nomination for the 2014 Nobel Peace Prize by Mr. Claes Nobel, grandnephew of Alfred Nobel, founder of the Nobel Foundation. This was the second time Len has been nominated for this prestigious award.

I asked Len to write a pilot's report that would provide insight about the Demon from someone who actually strapped it on and flew it into the sky. Len went one better, not only providing some of his own recollections about the aircraft, but also getting two more of his pilot buddies who flew the Demon to contribute as well. Len then compiled the stories and provided them in what he calls, "Demon Daze."

Thanks to Len and the others for adding so much to this publication. Their memories of the Demon provide a perspective of the aircraft that simply cannot be gained from any other source.

From Len Kaine

My very first recollections of the Demon were of McDonnell's F3H-1Ns which had the Westinghouse J40 engine. Westinghouse 'shoulda' stuck to toasters! The Navy had some of them barged down the Mississippi River from the McDonnell plant in St. Louis to NAS Pensacola where I was in preflight training in early 1955.

One of VF-61's F3H-2Ms is shown conducting carrier qualifications aboard USS FRANKLIN D. ROOSEVELT, CVA-42, in April 1957. At this time, the spoilers had not been added to the wings, and the detachable in-flight refueling probe had not become available for use with the Demon. Len Kaine was assigned to VF-61 when these qualifications were conducted and remained with the squadron the entire time it flew Demons. (McDonnell photograph from the collection of Don Spering)

This photo shows the four-ship flight of F3H-2M Demons from VF-61 that Len Kaine talks about in his narrative. In the firing area, the four pilots each took a turn at attempting to launch a Sparrow I missile at the target, but not one missile even fired, much less hit the target. Each of the four Demons returned to Oceana with their missile still on the launch rail. VF-61 never attempted to fire a Sparrow I missile again. (Photo courtesy of Bill Chaney)

Upon seeing those brand new F3H-1Ns, we all thought, "What beautiful blue Navy fighters are on the ramp by the old hangars along the NAS Pensacola shoreline!" The thing was, they looked great but couldn't fly! Later, McDonnell built the F3H-2M & -2N Demons with a bigger fuselage and greater wing area, and Allison fitted the J71 engine into the new birds.

I was commissioned and received my Naval Aviator Wings on 21 August, 1956, then checked into Fasron-5 at NAS Oceana shortly thereafter while waiting for orders to a fleet fighter squadron. I joined the "Jolly Rogers" of VF-61 in early 1957. We had the first F3H-2M day fighter Demons at NAS Oceana. After flying the non-afterburner F9F-8 Cougars and F3D Skynights in Fasron-5, the Demons were great!

William "Bucky" Goodman and I checked in at the same time. We were the most junior "Frapping New Guys" (FNGs) in the squadron. One day, the XO, Will Ennis, asked LT(jg) 'Burnie' Burnett where we were. Burnie told him Bucky and I were last seen together going over the horizon in burner, each fighting to take the lead. We were shooting high altitude gunnery while towing the banner at 20,000 feet.

Our training included low altitude strafing plus air-to-ground rocket firings and bombing with the small practice bombs. We also did a good bit of air-to-air combat maneuvering along with all the usual routine stuff on training flights. Wow!!!...for a young ensign to be in an afterburner-equipped day fighter was the best!

It was a stable platform for coming aboard and responded nicely to power changes. However, there were some restrictions on RPM minimums and the like. I especially liked the roomy cockpit with super visibility. Aboard ship at night we'd have dinner and then watch the movie while the night fighter F3H-2Ns were scaring themselves trying to get back aboard!

Then the problems started. Among other glitches with the J71 engines, in the super-cooled temperatures at altitude (in the clouds), the engine shroud would shrink and the compressor blades would grind to a halt, thus **flame-out-ville**. The joke was, "We were the only fighters that could be shot down with a water pistol. Argh!!! What they did (I can't believe I'm telling you this) was to shave down the tips of the compressor blades, so there went our thrust! Then they made up for the lack of thrust by adding some additional weight to the airplane, thus assuring it would be a dog! We used to joke that the plane captain would give you the signal to select afterburner while still in the chocks. He'd then run back and stick his head up the tailpipe, then come back forward with thumbs up indicating the afterburner was lit! Bad joke, but it was awful to be going backwards in performance.

Quick story... A good buddy of mine, Dick "Itchy" Koch, was flying the F3H-2N all-weather/night fighter Demons of VF-41. More of his comments are below. They had the all-weather AN/APG-51A radar with a scope to locate and track targets. By comparison, we had the AN/APQ-51A radar with only a small range indicator. It also fed ranging inputs to the gun sight. One day a group of us from VF-61 & VF-41 were doing some air refueling practice from an A-4 Skyhawk tanker. Dick plugged in and hung there while we waited (and waited) for our turns to refuel. Finally, Dick went into afterburner to push the drogue in far enough to get some gas. His comment was..."How Embarrassing!" and it was!

One day a division of us in VF-61 attempted to fire the Sparrow I missiles in our first, and what turned out to be our last, Sparrow shoot. Not a single missile even fired! That too was an embarrassment. The missiles on the rails looked awesome, but they were useless as a weapon. We were scheduled to carry Sidewinders but I never fired one from the Demon. I don't recall that we ever got Sidewinders before VF-61 was decommissioned.

We initially carrier qualified aboard USS FRANKLIN D. ROOSEVELT, CVA-42, and then conducted additional qualifications aboard USS SARATOGA, CVA-60, off "Gitmo," Cuba. Later we also had a longer at-sea period aboard the USS SARATOGA, officially called "Operation Strike Back," but it was frigid up there, and we sarcastically called it "Operation Blue Nose." It took us north of the Arctic Circle off the coast of Norway where the seas were rough and it was cold and windy. Fortunately there were no serious problems with our Demons, and, it was a thrill flying at low altitudes through the beautiful Fjords of Norway. During this time I was fortunate to make the 3,000th arrested landing on SARATOGA. We also did a "Cross Deck" operation with the British carrier HMS ARK ROYAL. It was fun stuff to have our Demons operating from their ship and the Hawker Hunters landing and launching from SARA. Later, the Brits had us over for a formal "Dining In"

31

An F3H-2M from VF-61 is hooked up to Cat TWO aboard SARATOGA during carrier qualifications. The "L" tail code indicates the squadron's short-lived assignment to Carrier Air Group SEVEN (CVG-7) (National Naval Aviation Museum)

while ARK ROYAL was at the pier near Portsmouth, England. It was the best Brit/Yank party I've ever seen. We also did a short period aboard the USS INDEPENDENCE, CVA-62, but it was quite tame compared to "Blue Nose" in the SARATOGA.

We had three Skippers during my two years in VF-61: CDR Joe Lovington, CDR Larry Budnick, and finally CDR Bob Hoppe. VF-61 was decommissioned in early 1959 and the day fighter Demons went "bye-bye". Skipper Bob Hoppe and I were the only two who transitioned to the F8U Crusader. The rest of our pilots went into F3H-2N Demons or got other orders to training command as instructors, to schools, or elsewhere.

The F8U was called a high speed one man transport, but it was one helluva gunfighter. I was a "happy camper" to be back as a VF-84 "Jolly Roger" in Crusaders. We convinced the VF-84 guys the "Jolly Roger" was too historical to let die, so we adopted it as our squadron insignia. It still lives today in VFA-103. Once again, it was great to be a "Jolly Roger" fighter pilot. And, as we used to sing at the O-Club Happy Hours…; *"We're the 'Jolly Rogers' ….Who the Hell are You?"* Luv to my brothers in Naval Aviation.
Len "Ski" Kaine

To continue, here are some stories from two other Demon Drivers.

First is Jim "Yank" Dorsey. Jim and I started Navy Flight Training as NavCads on the same day in 1955. We were roommates, squadron mates and shipmates. I was in his wedding and he was in mine. Friends like that are blessings. Twenty-nine years later his son, Tim, and my son, David, started Navy Flight Training on the same day in 1984. It was a pure coincidence but worthy of note. NavCad Jim retired as a vice admiral following a wonderful Navy career.

Here are some of his Demon memories…:

A week after I was commissioned Ensign USNR and fresh from advanced training at Corpus Christi, Texas, where I was awarded my Naval Aviator wings, I checked into my first fleet squadron, the "Jolly Rogers" of VF-61. It was the day before Thanksgiving 1956, and upon meeting the CO, he appointed me as the new Airframes Division Officer. He then introduced me to the squadron maintenance officer, Bob Cooke, my direct superior, who immediately invited me to his home for Thanksgiving dinner the following day. It was certainly a warm welcome I'll never forget.

VF-61 was typical of squadron manning at that time. The CO was Commander Joe Lovington, and the XO was LCDR Bill Chairs. There were three lieutenant Department heads, and the remaining fourteen, which included three ground officers, were ensigns and lieutenant junior grades. Only five of the nineteen were married, which made for terrific happy hours.

I was expecting to fly the F9F-8 Cougar, but I discovered the squadron was in transition to the F3H-2M Demon when the Operations Officer, Bill Franke, presented me with the Demon Pilot's Handbook (a book that described systems but nothing about how to fly the plane). I would have my first Demon flight early the following week. I then met Lee Clapper, the civilian McDonnell Aircraft representative, who walked me through a briefing on the

This rather unusual photograph shows the simultaneous launch of two of VF-61's Demons from USS SARATOGA during operations near Guantanamo Bay, Cuba. Note the splash in the water next to the ship. The two waist catapults did not have bridle catchers, so each time an aircraft was launched from one of those two catapults, the bridle went in the water, never to be used again. (Photo courtesy of Bill Chaney)

Demon's engine, hydraulic system, control surfaces, pneumatic system, landing gear, ejection seat, and other systems. That was followed by a session in the basic emergency procedures with Lee sitting on the cockpit sill. That was the extent of my training until the squadron XO, Bill Chairs, told me how to start and fly the Demon during a pre-flight briefing. The most unusual thing about the Demon at that time was the restriction not to retard the throttle below 91% RPM, because of the concern of having an engine stall below that point. That meant landing the plane was a bit touchy to keep it from landing too fast. The XO spent a lot of time in the pre-flight briefing emphasizing landing techniques, radio discipline, and emergency procedures. The latter was fortuitous.

After my very first afterburner takeoff, we spent an hour and a quarter doing formation flying, gunnery runs, and high speed maneuvering. This was exciting, and I greatly relished the high-G and speed workout. I thought, "Boy!! I have arrived." This was the F3H-2M day fighter version of the Demon, without the heavy, extensive nose radar of the F3H-2N. We had no external fuel tanks, no in-flight refueling probe, and no wing spoilers. These were added later and obviously had the effect of adding drag and weight to the plane. In any event, the Demon was still hot, very maneuverable, and great fun to fly.

VF-61 was very proud of the squadron's radio discipline, and throughout most of the 1.3 hours of my first flight, nothing was said over the radio by either of us. All info was passed by cockpit-to-cockpit hand signals. Today's young pilots will find that hard to believe. All was going great until we turned to head back to Oceana, then a red cockpit light came on. I had a hydraulic failure!

I should note that the Demon was a forerunner of using very high-pressure hydraulic systems for powering control surfaces on tactical planes. I recall that a previous Navy tactical jet, the F7U Cutlass, had a high-pressure system, but not as high as the 3,000 psi of the Demon. There were great growing pains in fighting the hydraulic leaks and pump failures, and here I had one on my first flight. Radio silence was broken. The XO calmly talked me through the emergency procedure for lowering my landing gear, flaps and ram air pump, and he told me I had to make an arrested landing. I guess I was just a dumb, naïve, green ensign who was too concerned about having broken the plane to be nervous or scared of the fix I was in. Oceana had a long stretch of various size anchor chains along side of runway 23. These were connected to a single cable across the runway that was held six inches or so off the runway by eighteen-inch sections of rubber auto tires. The fire crew rigged the wire with rubber tires across the runway in very short order. Without much ado, I landed as directed by the XO on my wing and engaged the wire for a stop. Chalk up my first jet arrested landing.

Much to my relief, I was not called to task for having broken the airplane.

VF-61 was a wonderful experience throughout. Our first carrier was the USS FRANKLIN D. ROOSEVELT, CVA-42, when we made an at-sea period for air-to-air gunnery training. I'll never forget being lined up behind CAT #1 and watching the Demon in front of me, flown by Art Benkelman, go into the water off the catapult. I was next to go off CAT #1, but the captain decided both the pilots and CAT officers needed more briefing, so he shut the operation down. Art was plucked out of the water without serious injury. After a few hours of stand down briefings we went back up to continue carrier qualifications. All went well until later when Will Ennis, our new XO, had an engine failure and went into the water in the wake during night qualifications. He also survived. It was said by an enlightened soul, "If I ever have to go into the drink in anything other than a tank I pray it's in a Demon."

The spoiler installation on the Demon was a much-needed fix, because without them the wings would warp in a high "Q" rolling stress environment. Prior to the spoilers being installed, McDonnell reps told us that the way to un-warp the wings was to accelerate to 400 knots, hold the top of the stick with the palm of the hand, and whack the stick with the free hand into the warp. Such was the state of aerodynamics in 1956.

Jim "Yank" Dorsey

And now over to Dick "Itchy" Koch who wrote:

I flew F3H-2N and F3H-2 Demons in two different squadrons. From April 1958 through November 1960, I was assigned to VF-41 at NAS Oceana, and from December 1960 through October 1962, I was with VF-101 in Key West. VF-41 was deployed aboard USS INDEPENDENCE, CVA-62, for both the ship's shakedown cruise and its first deployment to the Med in 1960.

The Demon was tremendously underpowered. On top of this, there was a period when there were a lot of flameouts or engine stalls when the aircraft entered clouds. As the problems were being addressed, various restrictions were placed on operations. At one time we were restricted to VFR flight conditions only. That's tough on egos if you are in an "all-weather" fighter squadron.

During another time period we were restricted from using afterburner except in an emergency. It was during one of these times of no afterburner use that we were getting ready to launch training flights from Key West. For some reason, the long runway, 07, was closed, and runway 13 was in use. It was 7,000 feet long with just marl at each end. There was no apron or overrun.

The weather was hot with not much wind. The squadron duty office had a nice view of the field, so a number of us gathered to see how much runway the first Demon would need for a basic engine takeoff. The Demon rolled and rolled, and it seemed as though it was not going to make it and would end up in the Atlantic Ocean. But at the last moment it rotated, barely getting airborne, and in the process created a huge cloud of marl dust off the end of the runway. After witnessing this takeoff, Demon flight ops were immediately canceled until runway 7 became available. We quickly referenced the performance charts which showed for the existing conditions, the Demon, in basic engine, needed exactly 7,000 feet for the takeoff roll!

The CAG F3H-2 Demon from VF-41 has multi-colored segments painted on its rudder. Dick "Itchy" Koch was assigned to VF-41 from April 1958 through November 1960. (National Naval Aviation Museum)

Some time in 1959, an Air Force F-102 squadron from Seymour Johnson Air Force Base was temporarily relocated to NAS Oceana while the runways at their home base were being resurfaced. I talked to one of their pilots at the 'O' Club during Happy Hour one day, and he remarked how impressed he was with the effectiveness of the Demon's wheel brakes. I asked him why he would say that. He said he was awaiting takeoff in the ramp area while a Demon was turning up on the runway, and the Demon was able to go into full afterburner without moving!!

The Demon was a very loud aircraft, generating many noise complaints from Virginia Beach residents. We felt if someone could develop a noise-to-thrust converter, many of our problems would be solved. This reminds me of a song we sang at the O-Club that ended..."I'm telling you boys, if thrust were noise we'd have a going machine."

I had my own experience with the compressor-stall problem. It was during a routine weekend navigational training mission to Otis Air Force Base on Cape Cod in the summer of 1959. Returning to Oceana on Sunday evening, I was being vectored by Otis Air Traffic Control for my climb-out in their operating area, so that I could enter into the FAA airways system at assigned cruising altitude. Otis was VFR, but there was a higher overcast. Climbing out in afterburner, I entered the clouds somewhere above 10,000 ft. and shortly thereafter I started losing power and noticed the gauges were showing indications of a flameout. In my state of panic, I forgot all about flameout emergency procedures which called for trying a re-light, and I remember continuing to push the throttle as far forward as possible. I told Air Traffic Control that I was experiencing a flameout, and they gave me vectors back toward the field as I descended. The engine stopped unwinding at 80%, and as I got lower I found I had regained control of engine speed with the throttle. I made a normal overhead landing back at Otis. I hitched a ride home with an Army pilot heading for Ft. Eustis in a twin-engine prop plane, and he was kind enough to drop me off at NAS Oceana. A few days later, I borrowed the NAS Oceana Beechcraft (SNB) and flew a couple of our mechanics and one of our pilots from the squadron maintenance department back to Otis. They gave the plane a few high-power turn-ups but couldn't find anything wrong. The plane was flown VFR back to Oceana without incident.

In the fall of 1959, VF-41 was embarked aboard USS FORRESTAL, CVA-59, to conduct the so-called Weapons System Evaluation Group (WSEG) tests off the east coast. The tests were designed to see if the carrier could defend itself in an all-weather electronic countermeasures (ECM) environment. Our Demons were outfitted with a new home-on-jam (HOJ) capability. All the flights were at night, and the attacking "enemy" was Strategic Air Command bombers operating lights out. VF-41 was the only fighter squadron on the carrier, and we were accompanied by a few A-4 tankers and some early warning aircraft. There was always a "ready" deck meaning we could launch and recover at will with no need to conserve fuel.

I remember using the HOJ feature which gave a bearing to the target, but you had to get in real close to pick the target blip out of the "noise" on the radar scope, if you could pick it out at all. On one run from astern the target, I called a "splash" and then passed the target in afterburner. As I did a wingover to look back, the bomber pilot had turned on all his running and anti-collision lights and looked like a Christmas tree. I must have gotten his attention! In the end, we proved that the carrier could defend itself, and we earned a lot of "atta-boys" from the powers that be!

At the end of November 1959, VF-41 was selected to represent ComNavAirLant at the Naval Air Weapons Meet (Top Gun). While most of the events were at MCAS Yuma, Arizona, the F3H competition was a Sparrow shoot over a period of several days at the Point Mugu missile range. Our team consisted of our skipper CDR H.C. MacKnight, LCDR Wayne McCord, and LTs Tom Cawley, Tom Ewall, and myself. As I recall, our opponent from ComNavAirPac was VF-53.

As the junior guy, I was designated as the spare for every flight and only got to go once. But I got a direct hit, scoring 100 on my only attempt and could brag that I had the high individual average for the event! Our team ended up winning the competition and flew to Yuma to collect our trophy.

A Demon from VF-41 is captured in flight in this photograph taken in 1961. Standard unit markings are evident and include a red flash with the squadron emblem on the fuselage behind the national insignia. The red fin cap and stripes on the rudder also adorned most of the unit's aircraft. Note the full missile loadout of Sidewinders on the inner pylons and Sparrows on the outer pylons. (U. S. Navy)

It's interesting to note that Len "Ski" Kaine was the ComNavAirLant Top Gun in the F8U Crusader and was the Navy's Top Gun at the same Naval Air Weapons Meet competition at MCAS Yuma. Two Marines had slightly higher scores using upgraded gun-sight radar tracking software which they chose not to share with the Navy. Inter-service rivalry is here to stay.

In the summer of 1960, aboard USS INDEPENDENCE, CVA-62, in the Med, VF-41 was involved in another effort to demonstrate that a carrier could carry out an assigned mission, this time by not being there. It seems that the Air Force had expressed doubt that the Navy could carry out its SIOP (Single Integrated Operation Plan) commitments. SIOP was the blueprint for the delivery of U.S. nuclear weapons in the event of war. To meet this challenge, the "Jolly Rogers" of VF-84 with their Crusaders and most of VF-41's Demons were repositioned to NAS Rota Spain. In their place CVA-62 took on a Marine A4D Skyhawk squadron and six more A3D Skywarriors, bringing the total number of A3Ds aboard to twelve. Left to defend the ship were four Demons with five pilots: Jim Dorsey, Gordo Murray (later to get command of an F-4 squadron as a LCDR), Bill Miller (who became a Grumman test pilot and died in an F-14 crash), Bill Everett (our LSO who died some years later piloting a private plane), and myself. Being the senior Lieutenant of those remaining, I was the O-in-C. (Funny how all the senior guys ended up in Rota!)

The Bay of Pigs fiasco occurred in April 1961. VF-101 was told to be ready in the event we were called upon to assist the invasion force. Of course, that never happened. However, all of our Demons were painted solid gray with no identification markings. That way, if we were called upon to get involved, no one would ever know they were U.S. aircraft.

NAS Key West was the center of activity during the Cuban Missile Crisis of October 1962. VF-101 in Key West was not much of a factor, because we were transitioning from Demons to the F-4 Phantoms in preparation for consolidating VF-101 Det. Oceana, the F-4 training squadron, with VF-101 Key West, which until then had been training replacement pilots for the F3H and F4D Skyray squadrons. Due to a shortage of staff at the Navy Flag Headquarters (Commander, Fleet Air Caribbean or some such) at the Naval Base near downtown Key West, VF-101 was tasked to provide officers to stand watches as needed, but that was about our only participation during the Crisis. I recall everything was micro-managed from Washington, including details such the uniform to be worn by Navy boarding parties.

A new medal was designed for the occasion, the Armed Forces Expeditionary Medal, and everyone who was attached to VF-101 at the time got one. We all wondered why, because we hadn't done anything. Since it was a brand new ribbon that no one had seen before, people would come up to us and ask what it was for. The standard answer was: "Oh that was for the battle of Dry Tortugas." (Dry Tortugas is the westernmost of the Florida Keys, sixty-five miles west of Key West with a national park and fort called Fort Jefferson.)

Dick "Itchy" Koch

For all you historians and enthusiasts with an interest in the early days of Navy jet Aviation, we hope you enjoyed just a taste of the wonderful memories from three old Fighter Pilots who have "been there and done that".

Len "Ski" Kaine

A DEMON RESTORATION

The beautifully restored F3H-2M is shown here with its wings extended at the National Naval Aviation Museum shortly after its restoration was completed. It is the best and most complete restoration of the three surviving Demons. (Kinzey)

Of the surviving Demons, the one that has been restored the best is the F3H-2M exhibited at the National Naval Aviation Museum at NAS Pensacola, Florida. For many years this Demon was displayed outside in the gate park at NAS Cecil Field, Florida. Even during that time, it was owned by the National Naval Aviation Museum and was on loan to NAS Cecil Field. When that facility was closed in 1999 during a series of base closures, the aircraft, which was in a deteriorating condition, was moved to the Museum for restoration. There it was painstakingly restored to the beautiful display aircraft that is available for all visitors to the Museum to see.

Most of the detail photos in the Demon Details chapter in this publication were taken of this aircraft, and it is because of the excellent work by the Museum's staff of volunteers that these excellent and extensive photos are possible. Their work is a tribute to their dedication to preserving the history of U. S. Naval Aviation.

The photos in this chapter show the F3H-2M from the time it appeared at NAS Cecil Field in the early 1990s up through how it looks today. Those taken during the restoration show the fine work done by the team that made it happen.

For the sake of accuracy, there are several anomalies that should be noted concerning this aircraft and its restoration. First, the Demon is F3H-2M, BuNo. 137078, which is one of twenty F3H-2Ms from production block j. The aircraft was displayed at NAS Cecil with that bureau number stenciled on its fuselage, and it was painted in the markings of VF-131, a Demon squadron that was based there in the early 1960s. However, VF-131 flew only the F3H-2N and F3H-2 versions of the Demon. At no time did the "Nightcappers" ever fly the F3H-2M. Taking this "liberty" is understandable, since NAS Cecil Field would want to display the aircraft in the markings of a unit that had been assigned there, and the specific version of the aircraft would not really matter that much for a "gate guard."

The National Naval Aviation Museum also painted the Demon using BuNo. 137078, and F3H-2M is lettered above the bureau number on the fuselage. However, the Museum chose to use the markings for VF-193 for the restoration. VF-193 also never flew the F3H-2M version of the Demon, so the markings on the aircraft as it is now displayed are not correct for any operational F3H-2M. VF-193 did fly both the F3H-2 and the F3H-2N after the latter had been upgraded to F3H-2 standards.

In restoring the F3H-2M, the instrument panel in the cockpit was rebuilt to the configuration used for F3H-2s and F3H-2Ns that were upgraded to F3H-2 standards. This configuration included the radar scope in the upper right area of the panel that was associated with the AN/APQ-51B radar. According to pilots who flew the F3H-2M, this scope was not present in that version of the Demon. However, the panel is a very accurate and well-restored version of the one used in the F3H-2, and photos of it are included in this publication to represent the one used in that variant as well as upgraded F3H-2Ns.

There are two other minor points to note about the restoration. First, the static pressure boom on the right wing tip has been shortened considerably. This is a safety measure to prevent visitors from accidentally walking into it when the aircraft is displayed with its wings in the extended position. Second, the entire underside of the horizontal stabilators is painted white. Photos of operational Demons show that approximately the inner half of each of the stabilators was painted with a heat-resistant silver enamel on the undersides.

The Demon on display at the National Naval Aviation museum is one of their many excellent aircraft that are preserved there for the public to see, enjoy, and study. The Museum is truly a national treasure, and it is highly recommended by Detail & Scale to everyone.

It should be noted that two other restored Demons are also on display at other locations. One is an F3H-2N, BuNo. 133566, which is part of the collection aboard the USS INTREPID, CV-11, Museum in New York City. The other is F3H-2, BuNo. 145221, displayed at the Pima Air & Space Museum in Tucson, Arizona, although at last report it was painted to represent F3H-2, BuNo. 143492, from VF-13 that operated aboard USS SHANGRI LA, CVA-38, in 1963. Therefore, one of each version of the Demon that reached operational service with the Navy is preserved.

We offer the following photos as a tribute to those who did such a superb job in restoring this part of the history of Naval Aviation.

F3H-2M, BuNo. 137078, was on display at the outdoor park near the gate to NAS Cecil Field, Florida, for several years. It was painted in the markings of VF-131, a squadron which flew F3H-2N and F3H-2 Demons from that air station during the early 1960s. This photograph was taken in 1991. (Kinzey)

After being moved to NAS Pensacola, the Demon began restoration by the National Naval Aviation Museum's excellent staff of volunteers. To start with, the outer wing panels were removed, and the aircraft was stripped of paint down to the bare metal. (Kinzey)

A lot of zinc chromate primer was used as an undercoat to help preserve the aircraft. The left main landing gear is shown here after the primer was applied. (Kinzey)

Right: The nose gear was basically intact, but it needed some cleaning and detail work. The lower UHF blade antenna had been removed from the left side door and was not replaced during the restoration. The location of the circular IFF antenna aft of the vents is visible, but the actual antenna is not present. (Kinzey)

At this point in the restoration, the outer wing panels had been removed leaving the inboard part of the wing fold hinge visible. The panels in the skin of the aircraft are also easy to see. Although the auxiliary inlet door, used with the Westinghouse J40 engine, was deleted when the change was made to the Allison J71, a triangular-shaped panel remained on the fuselage where the door had been located. (Kinzey)

This is how the F3H-2M looked with its wings folded at the National Naval Aviation Museum in May 2013. An Allison J71 engine is displayed with the Demon. (Kinzey)

A front view shows the F3H-2M as it was displayed at the Museum in January 2014 with the Allison J71 engine still displayed next to it. (Kinzey)

DEMON DETAILS
COCKPIT

Details of the instrument panel as used in the F3H-2 are shown in this view from the left side. This is also basically how the panel looked in F3H-2Ns that were upgraded to F3H-2 standards. The scope for the AN/APQ-51B radar often had a scope cover in place that made it easier to see in bright sunlight. Although Detail & Scale was unable to locate a NAVWEPS 01 for the F3H-2M, pilots who flew that version of the Demon report that the F3H-2M did not have the radar scope. Instead, the radar in the F3H-2M only provided ranging information to the gun sight. (Kinzey)

Additional details of the instrument panel are seen from the right side, including the armament control panel to the far left. The lever extending from the panel on the left side that has the round red knob on the end is the landing gear control lever. Basic items for the landing and take-off check lists are printed on the panel below the radar scope. (Kinzey)

Details on the aft end of the left console are visible in this view as is a good part of the seat back and bucket. Not all of the standard packing is on the seat. (Kinzey)

The throttle was among the items on the left console. It can be seen with a red button on top. The handle further aft of the throttle with the red wheel on top was the radar antenna hand control. Controls for the oxygen system are at the forward end of the console. The small gray lever on the side of the console next to the seat adjusted the friction for the throttle. Note the circuit breakers mounted high in the cockpit where they were in easy reach of the pilot. (Kinzey)

39

The small stick on the right console is part of the autopilot control panel. Most of the rest of the right console had controls for various electrical systems. These included the UHF radio control panel at the forward end, and the auxiliary radio receiver control panel just aft of it. Aft of the autopilot panel are the TACAN control panel, compass control panel, panels for the interior and exterior lights, and panels for the IFF and SIF systems. The large gray area is the map case. Again note the circuit breakers high on the side of the cockpit. (Kinzey)

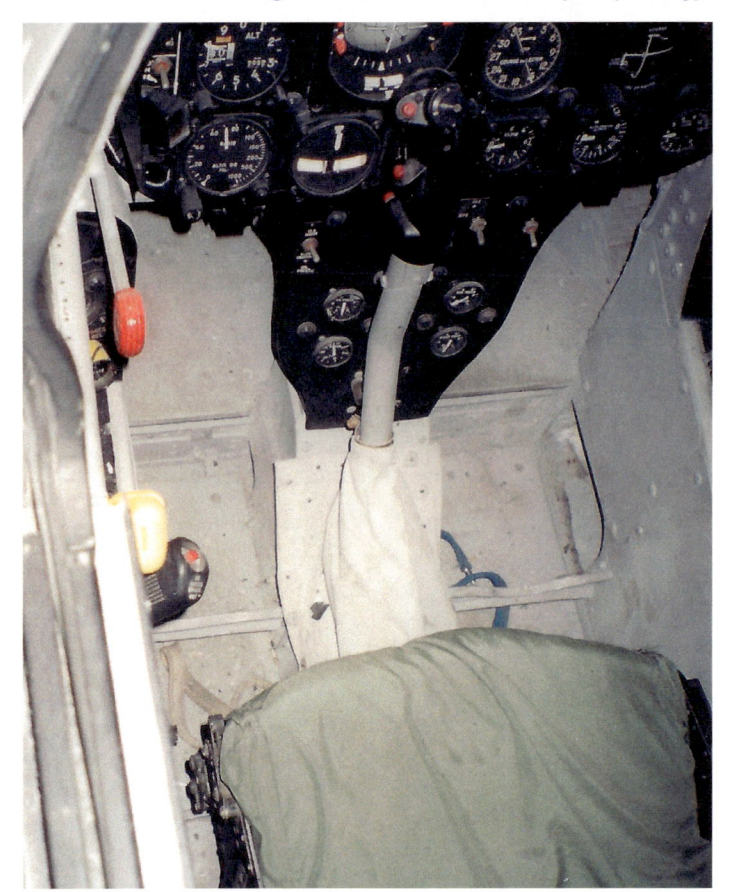

Part of the aft end of the right console can be seen here as well as the small oxygen bottle for the ejection seat. (Kinzey)

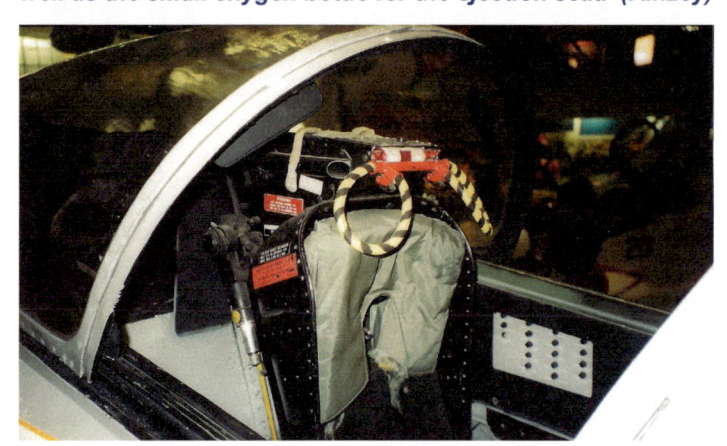

The ejection seat in this restored Demon is the Martin Baker H5 that became standard with the last production block of F3H-2 aircraft. It was also retrofitted to existing Demons, replacing the McDonnell seat. Details on the top of the seat are revealed here from the right side. To see additional details of the two ejection seats, refer to the drawings found elsewhere in this Cockpit Details Section. (Kinzey)

The cockpit floor is shown here along with the entire control column. (Kinzey)

Right: Another view provides a good look at the top of the Martin Baker H5 seat with its yellow and black face curtain rings at the top. (Kinzey)

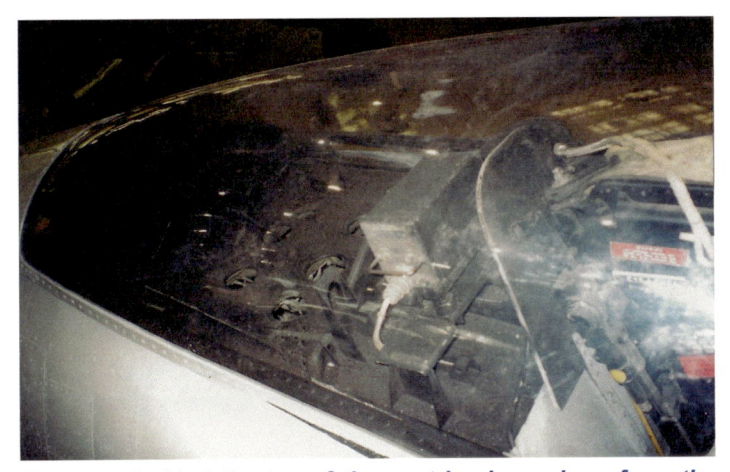

The area behind the top of the seat is shown here from the right side. There were relatively few details, and the area was painted flat black. (Kinzey)

From the left side of the aircraft, the area behind the top of the ejection seat is shown here again through the closed canopy. (Kinzey)

The drawings below, and those found on the following page, were created by Rock Roszak specifically for this Detail & Scale publication on the Demon. The ejection seat drawings are based on official drawings and photographs of the actual seats. The instrument panel, pedestal, and side console drawings are based on drawings found in the official NAVWEPS 01 manuals for the Demon.

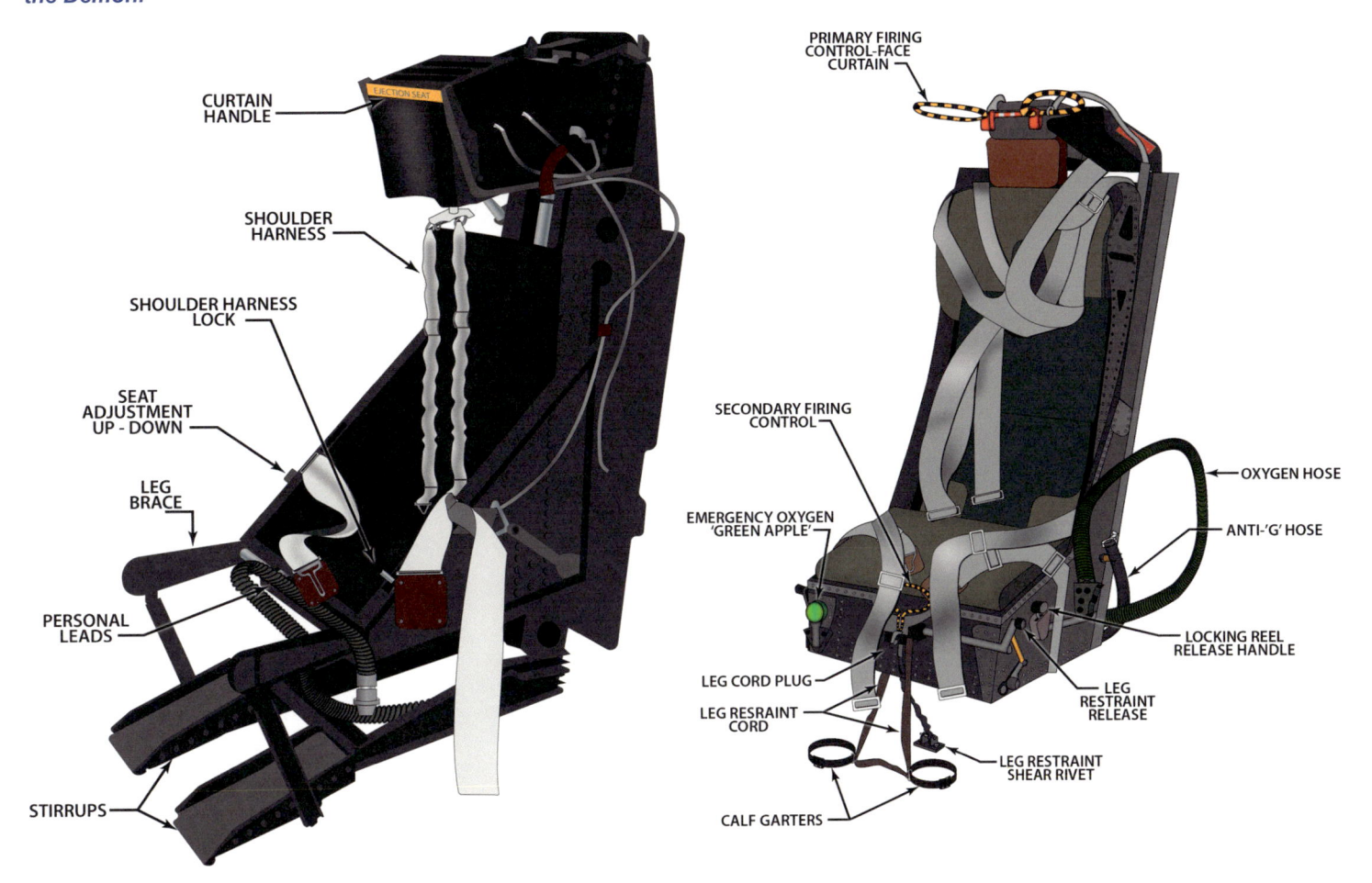

Originally, the Demon was fitted with an ejection seat that was designed and built by McDonnell, shown left above. This seat was initially installed in all Demons during production except for the last block of F3H-2s. Starting with BuNo. 146709, the McDonnell seat was replaced with the Martin Baker H5 seat on the production line, and the H5 was also retrofitted to existing Demons still in operational service. The Martin Baker H5 seat is illustrated at right above.

41

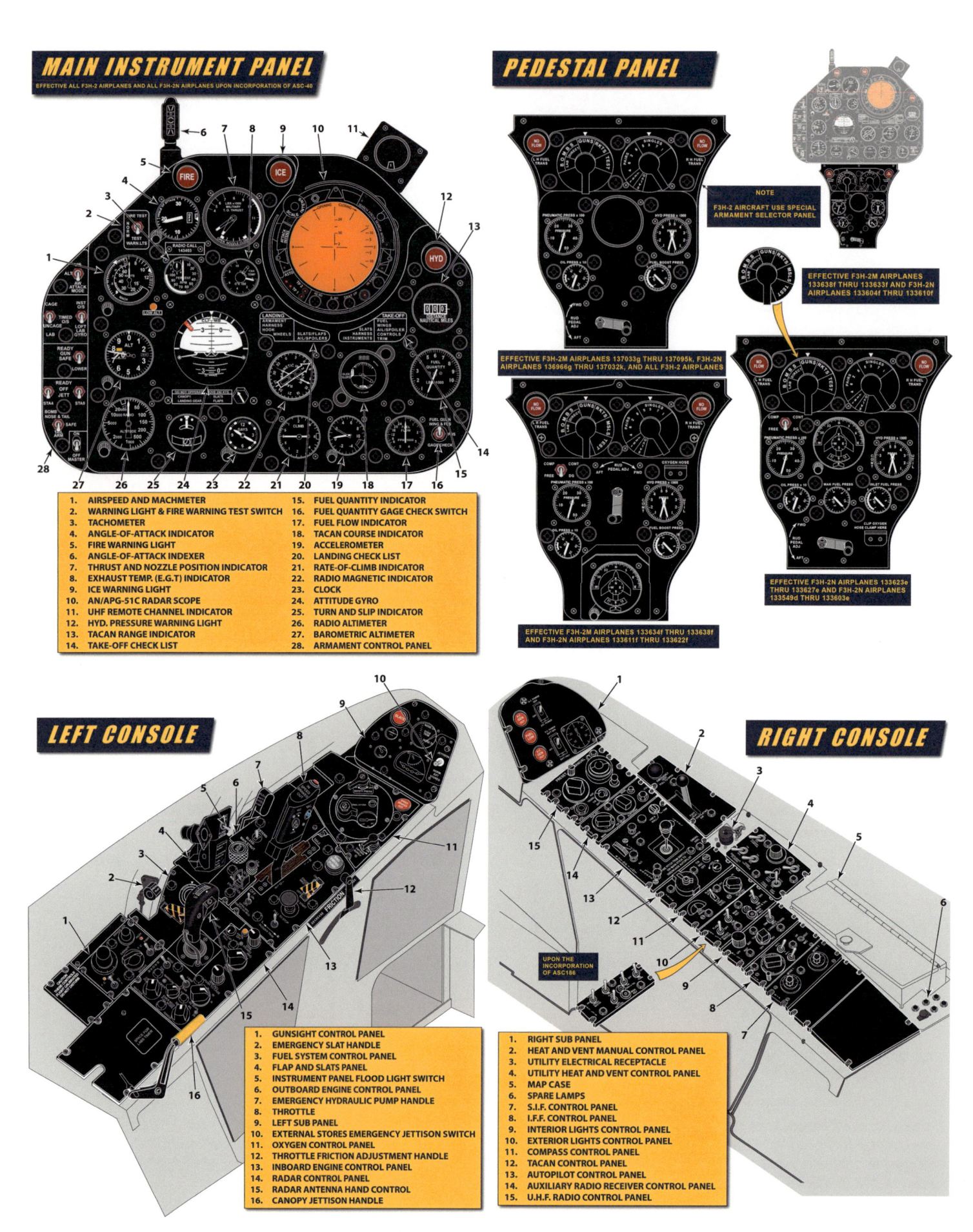

MAIN INSTRUMENT PANEL
EFFECTIVE ALL F3H-2 AIRPLANES AND ALL F3H-2N AIRPLANES UPON INCORPORATION OF ASC-40

1. AIRSPEED AND MACHMETER
2. WARNING LIGHT & FIRE WARNING TEST SWITCH
3. TACHOMETER
4. ANGLE-OF-ATTACK INDICATOR
5. FIRE WARNING LIGHT
6. ANGLE-OF-ATTACK INDEXER
7. THRUST AND NOZZLE POSITION INDICATOR
8. EXHAUST TEMP. (E.G.T) INDICATOR
9. ICE WARNING LIGHT
10. AN/APG-51C RADAR SCOPE
11. UHF REMOTE CHANNEL INDICATOR
12. HYD. PRESSURE WARNING LIGHT
13. TACAN RANGE INDICATOR
14. TAKE-OFF CHECK LIST
15. FUEL QUANTITY INDICATOR
16. FUEL QUANTITY GAGE CHECK SWITCH
17. FUEL FLOW INDICATOR
18. TACAN COURSE INDICATOR
19. ACCELEROMETER
20. LANDING CHECK LIST
21. RATE-OF-CLIMB INDICATOR
22. RADIO MAGNETIC INDICATOR
23. CLOCK
24. ATTITUDE GYRO
25. TURN AND SLIP INDICATOR
26. RADIO ALTIMETER
27. BAROMETRIC ALTIMETER
28. ARMAMENT CONTROL PANEL

PEDESTAL PANEL

NOTE
F3H-2 AIRCRAFT USE SPECIAL ARMAMENT SELECTOR PANEL

EFFECTIVE F3H-2M AIRPLANES 137033g THRU 137095k, F3H-2N AIRPLANES 136966g THRU 137032k, AND ALL F3H-2 AIRPLANES

EFFECTIVE F3H-2M AIRPLANES 133638f THRU 133633f AND F3H-2N AIRPLANES 133604f THRU 133610f

EFFECTIVE F3H-2M AIRPLANES 133634f THRU 133638f AND F3H-2N AIRPLANES 133611f THRU 133622f

EFFECTIVE F3H-2N AIRPLANES 133623e THRU 133627e AND F3H-2N AIRPLANES 133549d THRU 133603e

LEFT CONSOLE

1. GUNSIGHT CONTROL PANEL
2. EMERGENCY SLAT HANDLE
3. FUEL SYSTEM CONTROL PANEL
4. FLAP AND SLATS PANEL
5. INSTRUMENT PANEL FLOOD LIGHT SWITCH
6. OUTBOARD ENGINE CONTROL PANEL
7. EMERGENCY HYDRAULIC PUMP HANDLE
8. THROTTLE
9. LEFT SUB PANEL
10. EXTERNAL STORES EMERGENCY JETTISON SWITCH
11. OXYGEN CONTROL PANEL
12. THROTTLE FRICTION ADJUSTMENT HANDLE
13. INBOARD ENGINE CONTROL PANEL
14. RADAR CONTROL PANEL
15. RADAR ANTENNA HAND CONTROL
16. CANOPY JETTISON HANDLE

RIGHT CONSOLE

1. RIGHT SUB PANEL
2. HEAT AND VENT MANUAL CONTROL PANEL
3. UTILITY ELECTRICAL RECEPTACLE
4. UTILITY HEAT AND VENT CONTROL PANEL
5. MAP CASE
6. SPARE LAMPS
7. S.I.F. CONTROL PANEL
8. I.F.F. CONTROL PANEL
9. INTERIOR LIGHTS CONTROL PANEL
10. EXTERIOR LIGHTS CONTROL PANEL
11. COMPASS CONTROL PANEL
12. TACAN CONTROL PANEL
13. AUTOPILOT CONTROL PANEL
14. AUXILIARY RADIO RECEIVER CONTROL PANEL
15. U.H.F. RADIO CONTROL PANEL

42

WINDSCREEN AND CANOPY DETAILS

The windscreen and sliding canopy that comprised the cockpit enclosure on the Demon was unusual in that the windscreen was much deeper than the canopy. This provided excellent forward visibility that was praised by pilots and was very beneficial while flying an approach to landing aboard an aircraft carrier. (Kinzey)

Rather than having the canopy be as deep as the windscreen, the sides of the fuselage extended up as far as possible on either side of the cockpit. This allowed for a much smaller canopy aft of the windscreen. The low profile of the sliding canopy is clearly visible in this view. In spite of its lack of height, the canopy provided excellent all-around visibility for the pilot. (Roszak)

The first few F3H-2Ns were delivered with the same one-piece windscreen used on the F3H-1N. After a failure of one of these windscreens caused the loss of an early F3H-2N and its pilot, the windscreen was changed to a framed three-piece design with a bulletproof center glass. This design would remain unchanged for all subsequent Demon variants. (Roszak)

The three-piece windscreen is shown here from the right. The center section was flat, bulletproof glass. Note the silver tube at the base of the canopy with the small holes. Hot air was forced through the tube and out of the holes to defrost or de-ice the windscreen. (Kinzey)

On the first few early production F3H-2Ns, the pitot probe was mounted beneath the nose, but it was soon moved to this position at the base of the windscreen. All subsequent production Demons would have the pitot head in this location. The slot style air scoop just forward of the windscreen was the radar cooling duct. (Kinzey)

The clean, low, simple design of the sliding canopy is shown here from behind. The underside of the canopy that is exposed above the fuselage when open was painted a very dark gray. (Kinzey)

43

FUSELAGE DETAILS

All production Demon variants had the same radome regardless of the type of radar installed. The radomes were usually delivered in a semi-gloss black color, but they tended to fade considerably in service. (Kinzey)

This is the AN/APG-51A radar installed in an F3H-2N. The AN/APQ-51B of the F3H-2 was generally the same in appearance. The dish antenna for the radar was housed under the radome, which was hinged at the top for easy access to the antenna without removing the radome entirely. The associated power unit and other components were accessed through panels on each side of the nose section. (National Naval Aviation Museum)

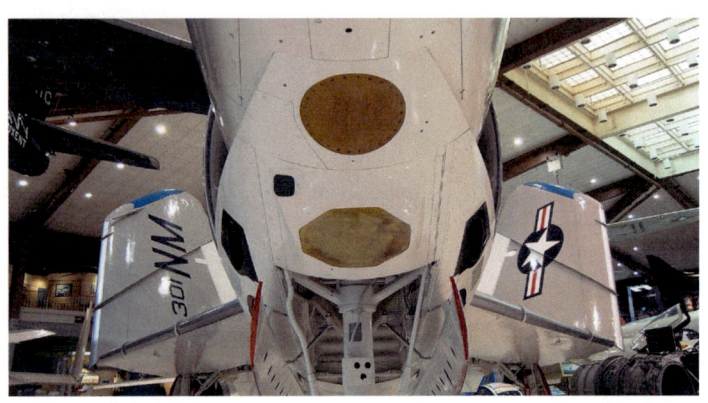

Three items were located in the area on the underside of the forward fuselage between the radome and the nose landing gear. The forward circular panel is the navigational TACAN antenna. Aft of it is the ultra high frequency Automatic Direction Finder (ADF) antenna panel. This antenna was present on F3H-2 Demons beginning with BuNo. 133611 and on F3H-2Ms starting with BuNo. 137041. The small item between the two antennas and to the left in the photograph is the gun camera. (Kinzey)

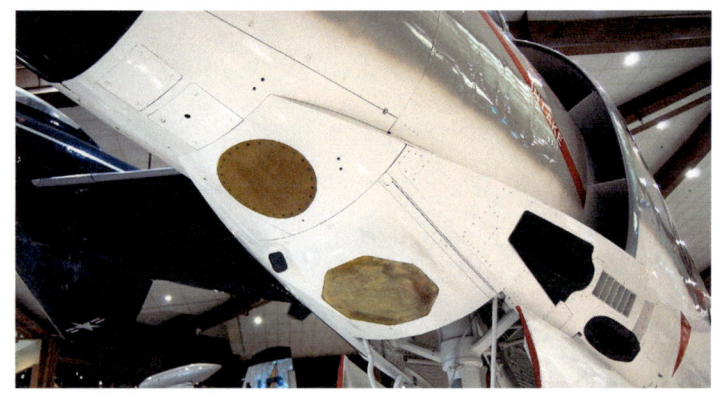

The same area is shown here again from a different angle. The small fairing for the gun camera is visible. Also note the small drain holes in various locations. (Kinzey)

The muzzle ports and vents for the two left side 20-mm cannons are seen here. While four cannons were standard for all Demon production aircraft, the two upper cannons were often removed in service to save weight on F3H-2Ns and F3H-2s. When this was done, their gun ports were covered with metal plates. In some cases, all four cannons were removed, leaving the interceptor armed only with missiles. (Kinzey)

The controls for operating the canopy from the ground were located just aft of the gun ports and slightly above the left nose gear door. It was simply a matter of pushing one of two buttons to open or close the canopy without having to climb on the aircraft. (Kinzey)

When the cannons were fired, the spent shells and belt links were discharged through chutes on each side of the lower fuselage just aft of the nose landing gear well. Outboard of the chutes there was a metal plate to help insure that the shells and links ejected down beneath the fuselage rather than fly out to the side toward the wing. *(Kinzey)*

The blast ports, vents, and ejector chutes for the two right side cannons are visible in this view. *(Kinzey)*

Taken from under the aircraft, this close-up shows the chutes for the shells and links for the two left side cannons. The aft end of the nose gear well is visible to the right. *(Kinzey)*

The cannons could be accessed through a large panel on each side of the forward fuselage. Ammunition boxes were mounted on a pallet, actually referred to as an elevator in the manual, which could be cranked down out of the aircraft for loading or replacement, then cranked back up inside the aircraft between the guns. Also note the ejection seat warning triangle in this photograph. *(Roszak)*

Air was fed to the Allison J71 engine through inlets on each side of the fuselage. These inlets wrapped around much of each side, but they were rather narrow. There were two dividers inside each inlet. This is the inlet on the left side of the fuselage. *(Kinzey)*

Left: This view of the right inlet shows that the interior was painted white. Also note the silver Corogard on the leading edge. The standard red jet intake warning chevron with white lettering was painted on each side of the fuselage forward of the inlets. *(Kinzey)*

45

A small formation light was located on each side of the engine inlets, and it was usually within the blue part of the national insignia. The lights on both the right and left side of the fuselage were identical and are shown above. (Both, Kinzey)

The single hook for the catapult bridle was located under the forward fuselage approximately even with the leading edge of the wing root. (Kinzey)

Taken from beneath the aircraft and looking aft, this photo provides a look at the location for the Automatic Direction Finding (ADF) Ultra High Frequency antenna on some aircraft. On many Demons, this antenna was located under the nose, but on F3H-2Ns, BuNo. 133611 and subsequent, and F3H-2Ms, BuNo. 137041 and subsequent, the ADF antenna was in this location under the fuselage. (Kinzey)

Although not originally designed with an in-flight refueling capability, a detachable refueling probe was quickly developed for the Demon. When used, it was attached on top of the right engine inlet as seen here. The black probe remained exposed even when in the retracted position. (National Naval Aviation Museum)

The refueling probe is seen here in the extended position as a Demon from VF-14 moves on to Catapult TWO aboard USS FRANKLIN D. ROOSEVELT, CVA-42. The probe worked with the Navy's probe and drogue in-flight refueling system. Although detachable, the probe unit was usually present on Demons once it was developed, especially when squadrons were deployed. (National Naval Aviation Museum)

46

This view shows the entire spine of the fuselage and reveals how it bows out and flattens beneath the vertical tail. Note that the upper red beacon is not mounted on the centerline of the aircraft, but is off slightly to the left side (Kinzey)

The small scoop mounted flush with the fuselage on the spine of the aircraft just aft of the canopy was the engine compartment cooling inlet. It is seen here from the right side. (Kinzey)

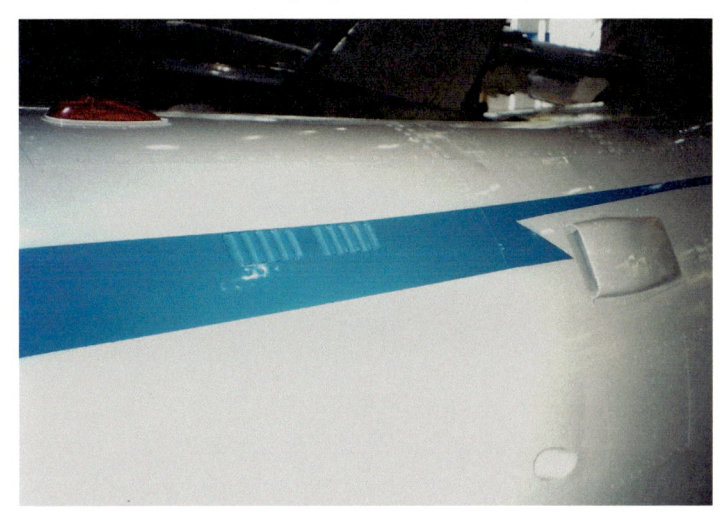

Several details on the middle section of the fuselage are seen here. The red beacon was mounted on the spine just to the left of the centerline. The series of vents is for the engine compressor, the scoop provides cooling air to the engine compartment, and the hole at the bottom of the photo is the compressor seal leakage duct. (Kinzey)

The same middle section of the fuselage on the left side of the aircraft is shown here from a different angle. The beacon light, compressor section vents, engine compartment cooling scoop, and compressor seal leakage duct are all visible in this view as well. (Kinzey)

In service, the exhaust from the compressor usually left a dark smudged area aft of it on the fuselage. The exhaust port can be seen above the Y in this photograph. Again note the scoop for the engine compartment higher on the fuselage. (Kinzey)

The items on the left side of the center fuselage are repeated on the right side. (Kinzey)

47

Two small scoops for the engine nozzle actuator ducting were located further aft on each side of the fuselage above the speed brakes. These are the two on the right side. (Kinzey)

The two small scoops for the engine nozzle ducting and the speed brake are shown here on the left side of the aft fuselage. The small access panel between the two hinges for the speed brake provides access to the arresting gear cylinder that moves the tail hook. There is one on each side of the aircraft. Below the hinges is the left side fuel drain for the fuselage tanks. (Kinzey)

The right side speed brake is shown here in the partially open position. The right fuselage fuel drain is also visible in this view. (Kinzey)

This close-up provides a look at the left speed brake in the partially open position. (Kinzey)

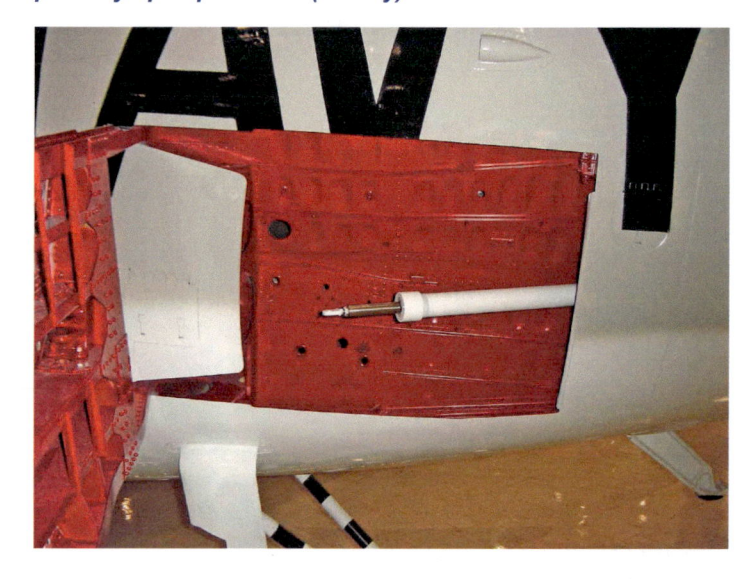

With the hydraulic cylinder detached from the speed brake, additional details of the brake and its well are visible. The brake was perforated with small holes and had considerable reinforcing structure on the inside. (Kinzey)

Right: Details inside the left speed brake well are visible here. Although the interior of the speed brake wells on this restored Demon are painted red, color photographs of operational Demons show that the wells were painted with a dark bronze-green or dark chromate green color. See the photographs on pages 28, 74, 75, 84, and 86 as examples. (Kinzey)

The Demon had a V-shaped arresting hook for carrier recoveries. Just aft of the hook was a tail bumper skid. Both the hook and the skid were hydraulically activated. (Kinzey)

From this angle, the small slot into which the tail skid retracts is visible. A small hydraulic cylinder is inside the slot, and it moves the skid between the extended and retracted positions. (Kinzey)

A close-up provides a good look at the retractable tail bumper skid in the extended position. It retracted into a well when the gear was retracted. The small item just to the left of the aft end of the well is the tow target release. (Kinzey)

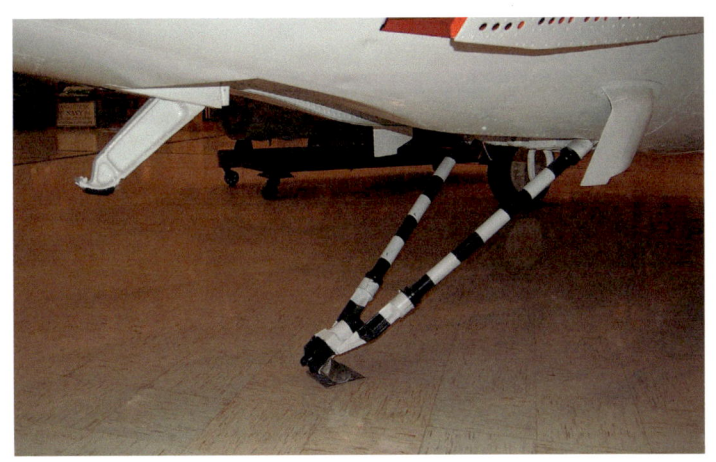

The arresting hook is seen here from the right rear. This photograph also provides a good look at the right fuel drain for the fuselage tanks. (Kinzey)

Details inside the tapered well for the arresting hook are visible here. The small link hanging down at the forward end of the well is for the catapult hold-back cable. (Kinzey)

The interior of the well for the tail bumper skid is shown here. The skid was L-shaped and attached to a hydraulic cylinder that retracted and extended it with the landing gear. Again note the tow target release to the left of the well. (Kinzey)

49

WING DETAILS

An overall view of the left wing reveals many of its design details. Noteworthy are the one long boundary layer fence and the three much smaller fences along the leading edge. Note the silver Corogard on the leading edge and the treatment of the non-skid walkway near the root. The walkway was applied in differing shades of flat gray and flat black on various aircraft. The raised spoiler is also visible. (Kinzey)

Looking outboard at the top of the left outer wing section, the thin boundary layer fence is visible. It is not quite full span, ending at a point just aft of the leading edge of the aileron and next to its outboard edge. In most cases, the national insignia was not painted on the fence as seen here, but photographs show that it was painted on the fences on some aircraft. (Kinzey)

The walkway was twenty-five inches wide and was usually gray, but flat black was also used. Specifications called for it not to be painted over the spoilers once they were added. (Kinzey)

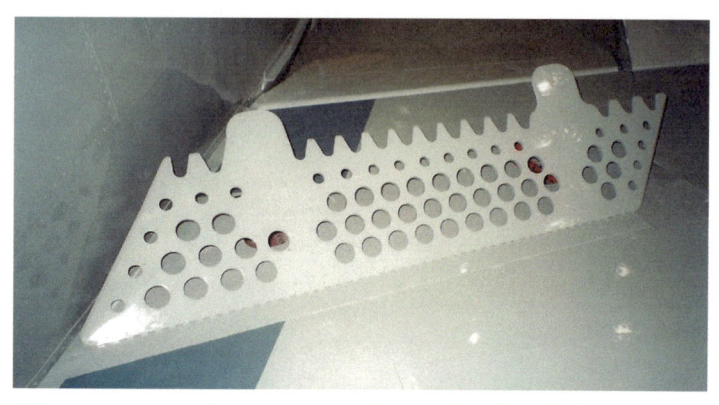

When wing warping was experienced during high roll rates, spoilers were added to the tops of the wings to spread out the forces. Although this added weight to the aircraft, it solved the warping problem without requiring a major redesign of the wing structure. This is the left spoiler shown in the fully raised position. Spoilers were standard on the F3H-2 and were retrofitted to the F3H-2N and F3H-2M variants. (Kinzey)

The left spoiler is shown here from behind in the fully raised position. Two hydraulic cylinders actuated the spoiler. Note that there is no well in the wing. Instead the spoiler rested flat on top of the wing when in the down position. As with speed brakes, the inside surface was painted red. (Kinzey)

The left spoiler is shown again from behind, but this time it is in the lowered position. Note how it rested on top of the wing surface. The raised area of the spoilers caused drag, and their weight also reduced the performance of the Demon, but they were necessary to eliminate the warping problem. (Roszak)

50

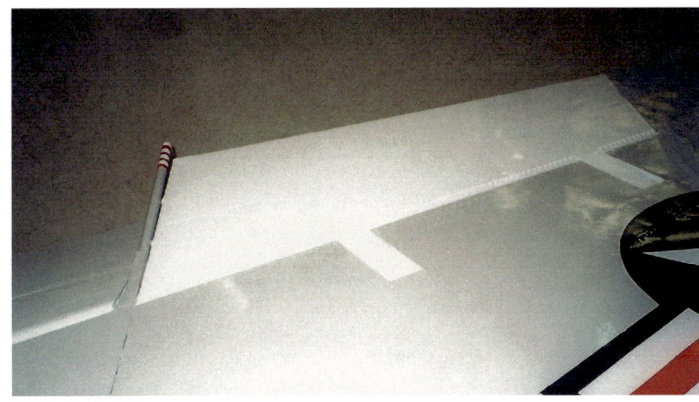

Roll control was initially provided only by ailerons, each of which was attached to the structure of the outer wing sections by two large hinges. Both the upper and lower surfaces of the ailerons were painted white. After the spoilers were added, they combined with the ailerons to provide roll control. (Kinzey)

A fuel dump tube for the wing tanks was located between the flap and aileron on each wing. This is the fuel dump tube for the left wing tanks. (Kinzey)

Leading edge slats provided extra lift when the Demon was flying at slow speeds during takeoffs and landings. They were hydraulically operated, and they remained closed when the aircraft was on the ground. There were three small fences on the leading edge of the wing in addition to the large boundary layer fence. Two are shown in this view. (Kinzey)

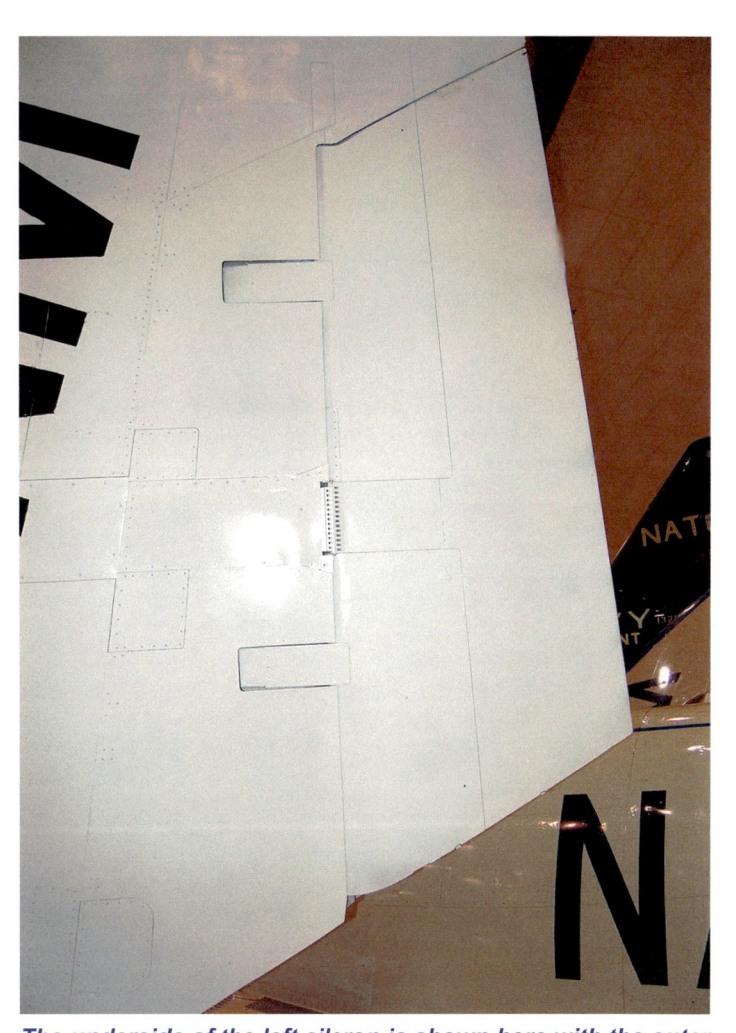

The underside of the left aileron is shown here with the outer wing section in the folded position. (Kinzey)

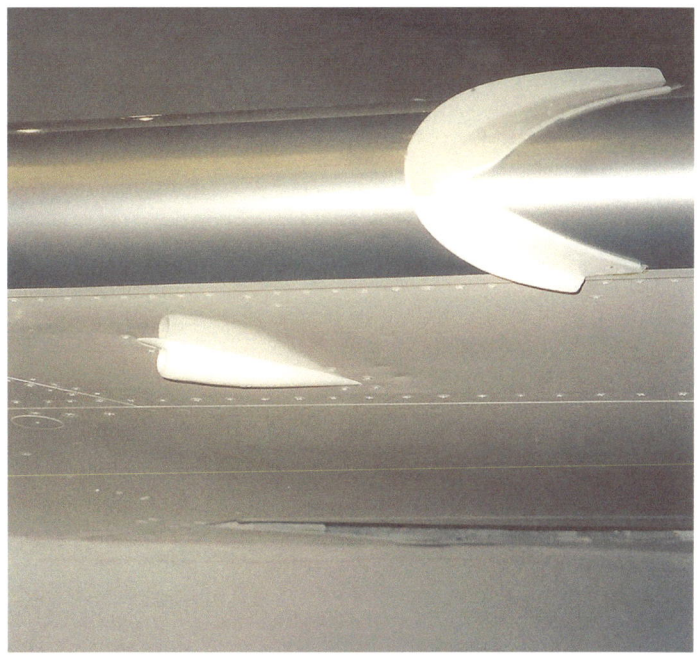

A small scoop was located under each wing near the leading edge. It was part of the fuel system sub-assembly that regulated the fuel pressure differential within the fuel tanks located in the wing. This is the scoop under the left wing. (Kinzey)

51

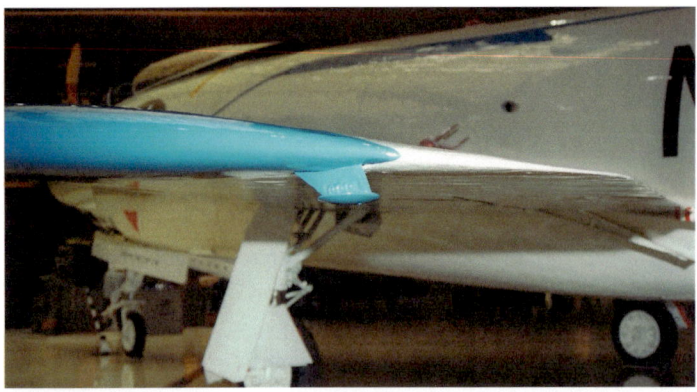

A small wing tip skid was mounted at the trailing edge of each wing tip. (Kinzey)

At the forward point of the wing fold, the cross-section of the leading edge slat can be seen against the main wing structure. (Kinzey)

The wing fold hinge for the left wing is shown here from the inside. (Kinzey)

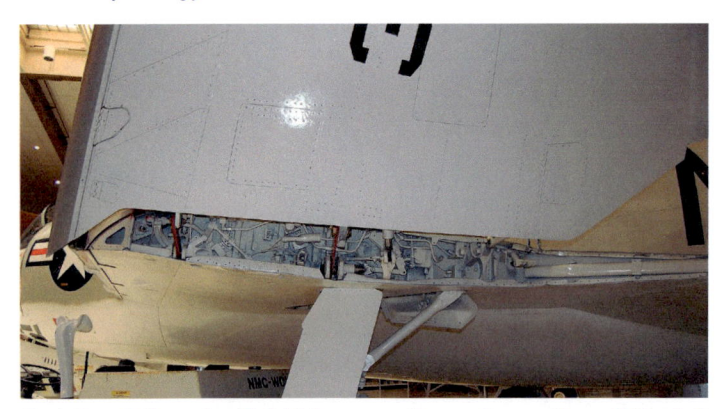

Details of the wing fold hinge on the main section of the left wing can be seen here. (Kinzey)

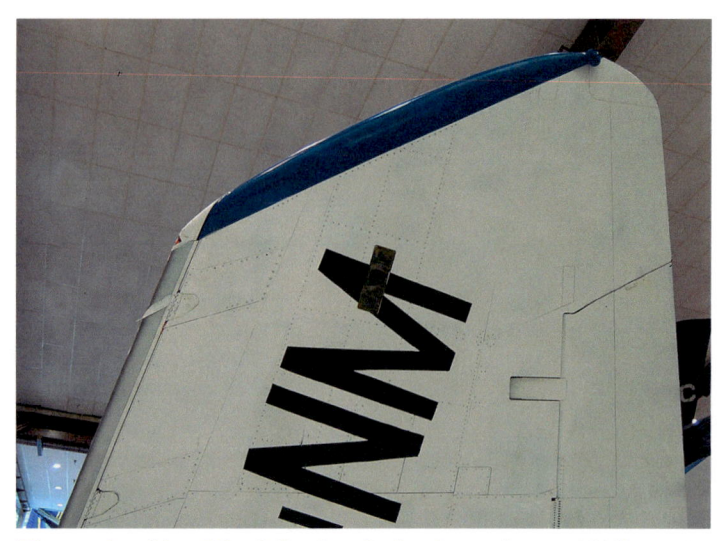

The underside of the left wing tip is shown here with the outer wing section in the folded position. The small red position light is visible on the leading edge of the tip. Note again the wing tip skid. The small rectangle in the "M" is the receiver-transmitter for the radar altimeter. (Kinzey)

A low view looks up at the wing fold hinge on the left outer wing panel. (Kinzey)

The aft end of the wing fold interior on the center section of the left wing shown here with the wing fuel drain tube running inside it and out past the flap. (Kinzey)

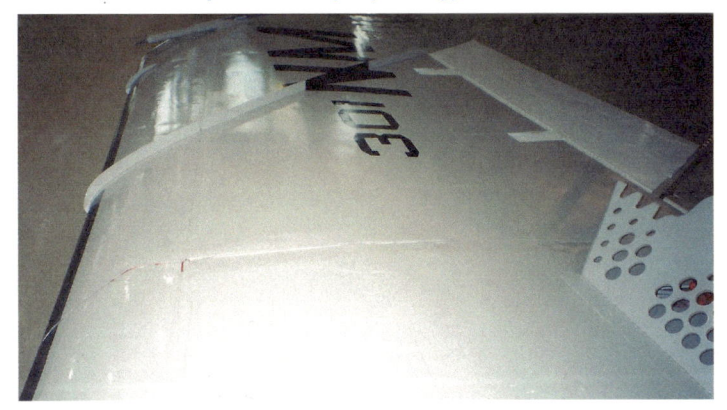

Looking outboard along the top of the right wing reveals the boundary layer fence and the aileron. The static pressure boom on this aircraft was shortened considerably to prevent injury to visitors at the National Naval Aviation Museum. (Kinzey)

A high view provides a look at the three control surfaces on the right wing. The wing spoiler is in the raised position, and the flap is lowered a few degrees. The aileron was mounted on the folding section of the wing, but it was not full span. As was standard practice on the Light Gull Gray over white paint scheme, both upper and lower surfaces of the flaps and ailerons were painted white. (Kinzey)

Right: The wing tips on the Demon were an unusual design. The cap on the tip was not full chord in length as can be seen here. Instead, the aft end of the trailing edge was rounded to meet the tip. Note that the wing fence is in line with the outer edge of the aileron. (Kinzey)

A top view of the right wing shows the silver Corogard and the three small fences in the leading edge. These small fences were desgined to catch the vertical strips of the barrier during a barrier recovery aboard an aicraft carrier. The spoiler is in the raised position. Note that the painted walkway is not flush against the side of the fuselage. (Kinzey)

53

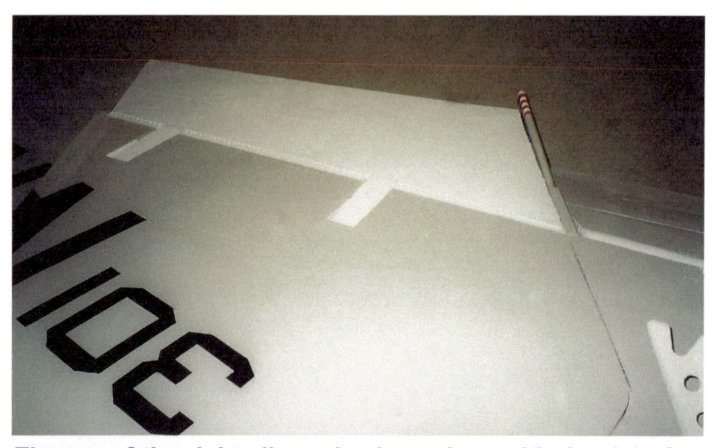

The top of the right aileron is shown here with the right fuel dump tube immediately inboard of its edge. (Kinzey)

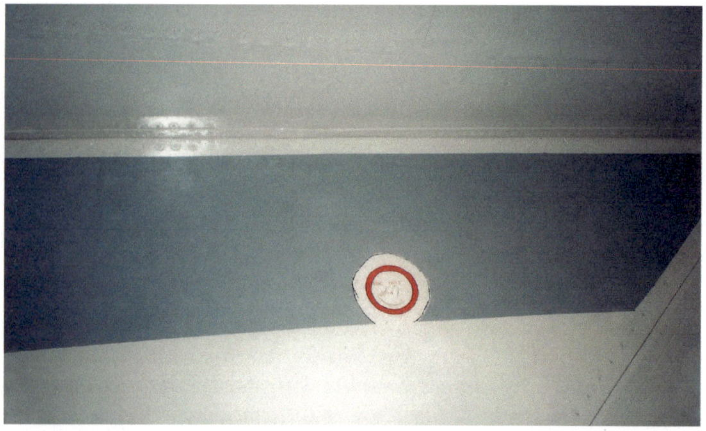

A fill location for the wing tanks was located near the wing root and within the walkway area of each wing. (Kinzey)

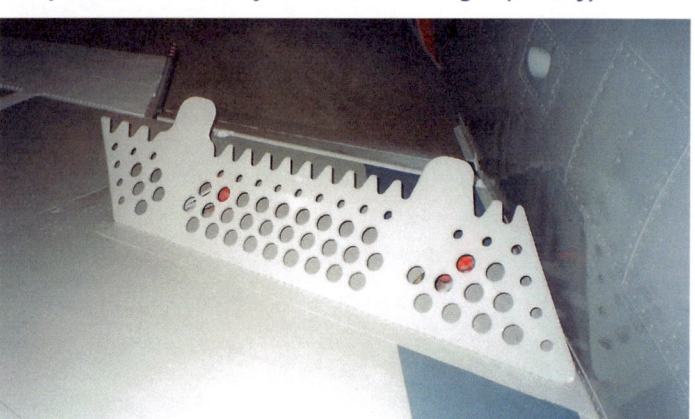

The right spoiler was a mirror image of the one on the left wing. (Kinzey)

The right wing spoiler is shown in the raised position from behind. (Kinzey)

In this view, the right wing spoiler has been lowered to the closed position. (Roszak)

With the wing folded, it is possible to see how the right fuel dump tube extends forward between the inner and outer wing sections. However, a section of the tube that runs into the wing structure is missing on this restoration. The right flap can also be seen in the slightly lowered position. (Kinzey)

Left: The right fuel dump tube is shown here from the inside next to the flap. The red and white stripes helped to make the tube more visible when the wing was folded and the flaps were lowered. (Kinzey)

The underside of the right outer wing section is revealed here. No antennas were located on this wing panel. (Kinzey)

The right wing fold line can be seen in this photograph taken from the cockpit. (Kinzey)

Details of the wing fold hinge on the center wing section of the right wing are illustrated in this view. (Kinzey)

Although it appears to be blue, the green position light can be seen on the leading edge of the right wing tip. Also visible in this photograph are the attachment point for the static pressure boom and the wing tip skid at the trailing edge. (Kinzey)

Left: Looking up at the right wing fold hinge reveals the details on the outer wing section. The wings on the Demon were folded hydraulically. (Kinzey)

55

PYLONS, MISSILE RAILS, & EXTERNAL STORES

A Demon assigned to VF-161 shows the most common pylon and missile rail combination used on F3H-2s and F3H-2Ns after the latter were upgraded to F3H-2 standards to employ the Sparrow III missile. The inboard pylon has an AERO 1A launch rail for the Sidewinder missile. Note how the rail extends forward and aft of the pylon. The pylon used for the AERO 1A was shorter in chord than the one used with the AERO 3A launch rail for the Sparrow I and the AERO 4A launcher for the Sparrow III, and this can be seen by comparing the inboard pylon with the outboard pylon in this photograph. On the outboard pylon is an Aero 4A launch rail used for the Sparrow III. Note that the AERO 4A launch rail is blue, as was often the case for both AERO 3A and AERO 4A launchers, and it has an orange inlet on top of the forward end. Also note that the aft end of the launch rail is slightly tapered and is flush with the trailing edge of the pylon. In most cases when both Sidewinders and Sparrow IIIs were carried, the Sidewinder was mounted inboard and the Sparrow III outboard as shown here. However, the mounting was reversed at times. (National Naval Aviation Museum)

We are including a special section on the pylons and launch rails for Sidewinder and Sparrow missiles used on the Demon. Particular emphasis is needed here, because most references have this wrong, and modelers should note that these features are often inaccurate or totally incorrect in scale model kits. Each missile had its own specific launch rail and each was different. Further, as pointed out in the Demon Variants chapter of this book, each version of the aircraft could carry specific types of missiles but not others. All three operational variants could employ the Sidewinder once it became available, but only the F3H-2M could employ the Sparrow I. The Sparrow III could only be carried by the F3H-2 version as well as the F3H-2Ns that were later upgraded to F3H-2 standards.

The purpose of this section is to illustrate and explain the correct use of the missiles and their launch rails for each Demon variant.

The presence of the AERO 4A launcher for the Sparrow III missile on the outboard pylon of this F3H-2N indicates that it has been upgraded to F3H-2 standards. But note that it retains its original long beaver tail. Contrary to what has been reported elsewhere, the upgrade did not include replacing the long beaver tail with the short one. In this case, the AERO 4A launcher has blue forward and aft sections, but most of it is a dark metallic gray color. This was often seen on AERO 4A launchers, but it was not as common as the overall blue color. Again, note the orange inlet on top of the forward end of the launch rail. From this direct side view, the shorter chord of the pylon for the AERO 1A launch rail, used with the Sidewinder missile, is evident. The AERO 1A is fitted to the inboard pylon, and a training version of the Sidewinder missile is loaded. (National Naval Aviation Museum)

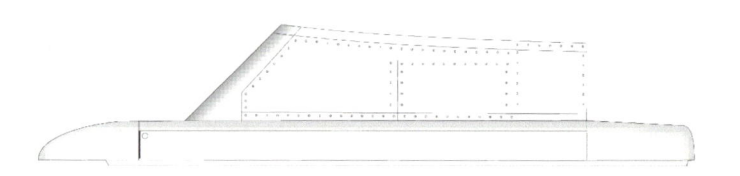

Details of the pylon and the AERO 1A launch rail used for the AAM-N-7A (AIM-9B) Sidewinder missile are revealed in this artwork. Note that the launcher extended fore and aft of the pylon, and that both ends of the rail were curved. AERO 1A launch rails were almost always painted white. While F3H-2Ms were able to carry the Sidewinder missile, the service life of that version of the Demon was relatively brief, and by the time the Sidewinder became operational, F3H-2Ms were about to be withdrawn from service. Therefore, it is fairly uncommon to see Sidewinder launch rails and missiles on F3H-2Ms. (Artwork by Rock Roszak)

BuNo. 133569 was the first F3H-2M built, and it served as the prototype for this Demon variant. It is shown in this publicity photograph with four inert Sparrow I missiles under its wings. The AERO 3A launch rail for the Sparrow I missile had an angular leading edge, and the aft end mounted flush with the trailing edge of the pylon. Note how far aft the missile extended beyond the trailing edge of the launch rail and how little the front of the missile extended forward of the rail. The AERO 3A was quite different from the AERO 4A used with the Sparrow III missile, and it had no inlet on top of the forward end. Almost all AERO 3A launch rails were painted blue, but photos show that those used on F3H-2Ms at Point Mugu were exceptions, being painted white. (McDonnell photograph from the collection of Don Spering)

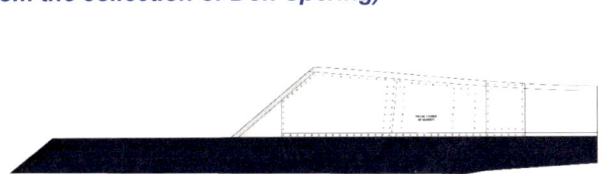

This illustration reveals the simplicity of the AERO 3A launch rail used on the F3H-2M for the Sparrow I missile. It was basically a straight rail with an angular leading edge and vertical trailing edge. Up to four pylons with AERO 3A launchers could be carried on an F3H-2M. These would be attached to stations 1, 3, 6, and 8. It should be re-emphasized that the AERO 3A launch rails and the Sparrow I missile were used only with the F3H-2M version of the Demon. (Artwork by Rock Roszak)

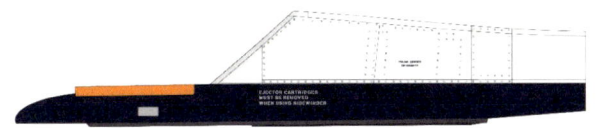

The AERO 4A launch rail used with the Sparrow III missile was more complex than the AERO 3A used with the Sparrow I. It had an inlet on top of the forward end, and this was usually painted a dark orange color. The rear part of the rail was slightly tapered on the bottom, and the aft end mounted flush with the trailing edge of the pylon. While many AERO 4A launchers were Sea Blue in color, some had a dark metallic center section with blue end pieces, while a few were painted white. (Artwork by Rock Roszak)

This F3H-2 from VF-31 has an AERO 1A launch rail with a training version of the Sidewinder missile on the pylon mounted to station 3, and an AERO 4A launcher with the body of a SPARROW III missile on station 1. Note the differences in the two launch rails, and notice how the aft end of the AERO 4A is tapered slightly, providing increasing separation from the missile body. This loading arrangement was the most common when both Sidewinders and Sparrow IIIs were carried. (National Naval Aviation Museum)

The F3H-2N on display at the Intrepid Sea, Air, and Space Museum had AERO 4A launch rails for Sparrow III missiles on stations 1, 3, 6, and 8, when this photo was taken. While it was possible for the F3H-2 and upgraded F3H-2Ns to carry four Sparrow III missiles at one time, photographic evidence indicates that this was seldom, if ever, done. Whenever four missiles were carried, it was almost always a combination of two Sparrow IIIs and two Sidewinders. (Kinzey)

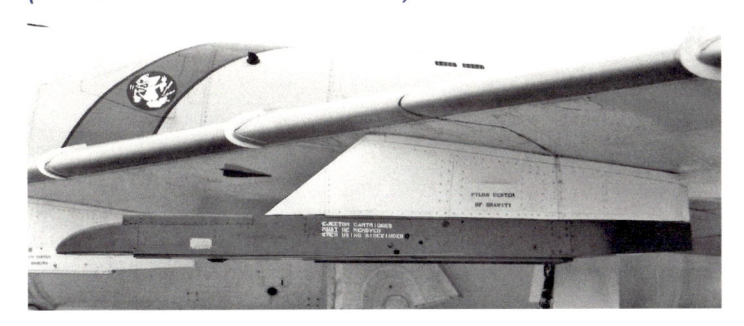

Left: A close-up photograph provides a good look at the details of the AERO 4A launcher on station 1 of the Demon displayed at the Intrepid Sea, Air, and Space Museum. (Kinzey)

An F3H-2 from VF-14 has its launch rails mounted opposite of the more common arrangement seen on F3H-2 and upgraded F3H-2N versions of the Demon. In this case the AERO-1A rail with the Sidewinder missile is mounted on the outboard station, while the AERO 4A launcher for the Sparrow III missile is on the inboard station. While not as common as the opposite loading, this arrangement was seen in operational use. (National Naval Aviation Museum)

This in-flight view of F3H-2N, BuNo. 133572, shows the aircraft with four 2.75-inch rocket pods in place on stations 1, 3, 6, and 8. These rocket pods could be used to augment the 20-mm cannons and missile armament in the air-to-air role, and they could also be used against ground targets. While the use of these rocket pods was quite common on the F4D-1 Skyray as an air-to-air weapon, they were used far less frequently on the Demon. Although this photo shows two of the 282-gallon fuel tanks under the fuselage, this was seldom done operationally, because the drag of the two tanks more than negated the benefit of the extra fuel, thus reducing range when they were both carried. (McDonnell photograph from the collection of Don Spering)

Right: Two large pylons could be mounted under the fuselage of the Demon. The most common external store carried on these pylons was a 282-gallon fuel tank as shown on station 4 in this photograph. Usually only one tank was carried, and the use of even one external fuel tank was relatively limited. This was because carrying two tanks actually reduced range due to the increased drag of the tanks. Using one tank provided only a marginal increase in range. In addition to the fuel tank, any store heavier than 500 pounds were also carried on these fuselage pylons, because the wing stations were limited to 500 pounds or less. When carried, the self-contained starter unit was loaded on the right fuselage pylon, station 5. (National Naval Aviation Museum)

It should be noted that a rectangular pylon was also used on the six wing stations on all versions of the Demon, including the F3H-1N. It was the only pylon that could be mounted on the center wing stations, 2 and 7. This rectangular pylon was used to carry rocket pods and air-to-surface weapons. The lead F3H-2N in this photo has AERO 7D rocket pods for nineteen 2.75-inch rockets on its inboard stations. Smaller AERO 6A rocket pods, each carrying seven 2.75-inch rockets are mounted on the mid-wing pylons on stations 2 and 7. The 2.75-inch rockets could be used against both aerial and surface targets. 500-pound bombs are on the outboard stations. The other two Demons have AERO 7D rocket pods on stations 1, 3, 6, and 8, while small Mk 76, 25-pound practice bombs are on stations 2 and 7. The pylons are painted blue on these aircraft, but many of these rectangular pylons were white. (National Naval Aviation Museum)

F3H-2N, BuNo. 137029, is loaded with bombs, demonstrating the Demon's capability as a fighter-bomber, a role that was secondary to that of fleet defense interceptor. The Sea Blue wing pylons are loaded with 250-pound general-purpose bombs, and 1,000-pound bombs are mounted on the two fuselage pylons. Each of the wing pylons could carry stores weighing up to 500 pounds, and the two fuselage pylons could carry stores up to 2,000 pounds in weight. However, the total weight of external stores could not exceed 4,000 pounds. (Spering)

58

This illustration shows a 282-gallon external fuel tank attached to one of the fuselage pylons. While any external store weighing more than 500 pounds was to be carried on one of the fuselage racks, these fuel tanks are the only stores seen on them with any regularity in photographs. On rare occasions, the self-starter unit was attached to one of these pylons, but we have found no photographic evidence that any large weapons were carried on them operationally. Those that were carried on one of the fuselage stations appear to have been for evaluation or display purposes only. (Artwork by Rock Roszak)

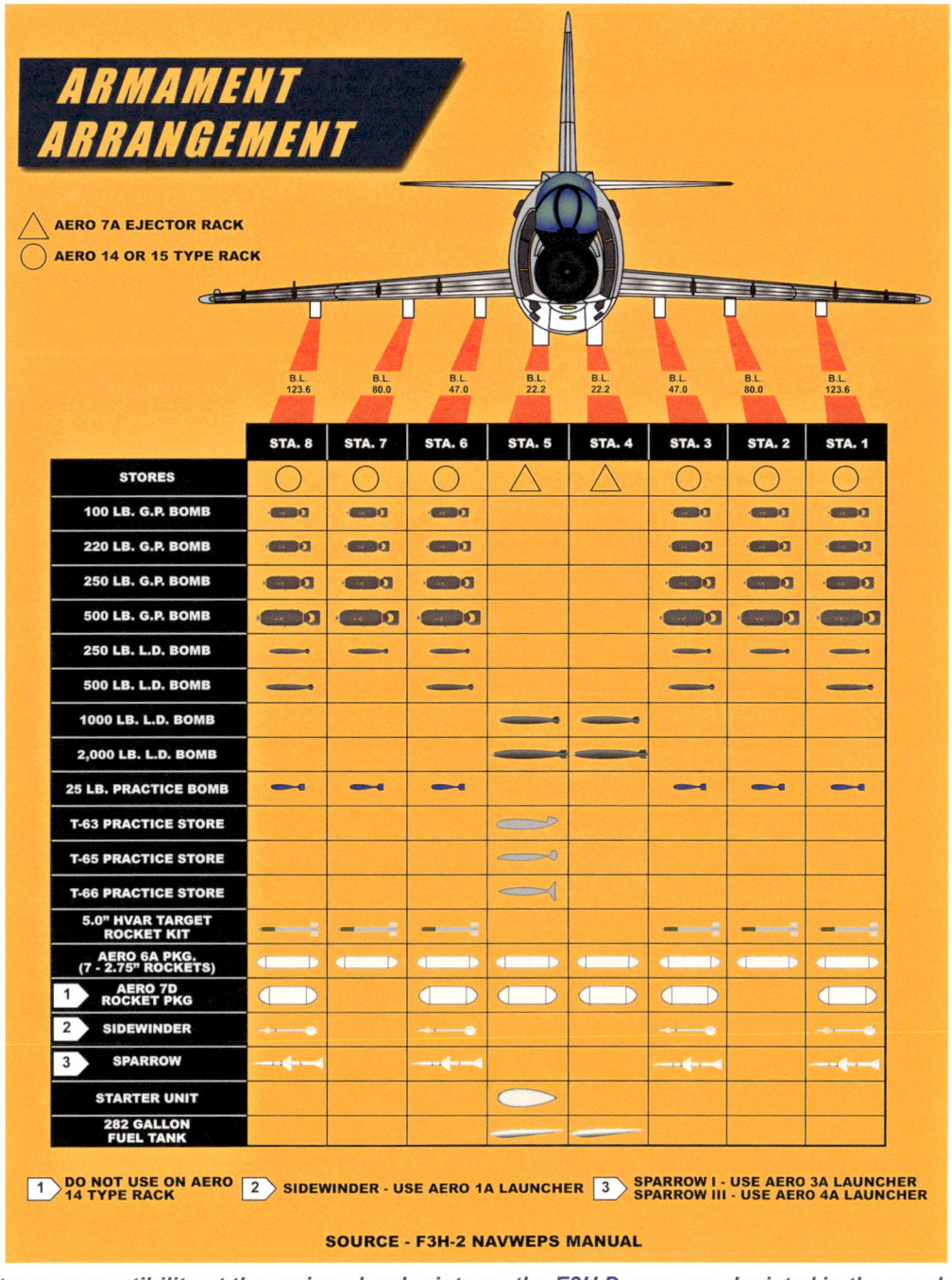

ARMAMENT ARRANGEMENT

△ AERO 7A EJECTOR RACK
○ AERO 14 OR 15 TYPE RACK

STORES	STA. 8 (○)	STA. 7 (○)	STA. 6 (○)	STA. 5 (△)	STA. 4 (△)	STA. 3 (○)	STA. 2 (○)	STA. 1 (○)
B.L.	123.6	80.0	47.0	22.2	22.2	47.0	80.0	123.6
100 LB. G.P. BOMB	●	●	●			●	●	●
220 LB. G.P. BOMB	●	●	●			●	●	●
250 LB. G.P. BOMB	●	●	●			●	●	●
500 LB. G.P. BOMB	●	●	●			●	●	●
250 LB. L.D. BOMB	●	●	●			●	●	●
500 LB. L.D. BOMB	●	●	●			●	●	●
1000 LB. L.D. BOMB				●	●			
2,000 LB. L.D. BOMB				●	●			
25 LB. PRACTICE BOMB	●	●	●			●	●	●
T-63 PRACTICE STORE				●				
T-65 PRACTICE STORE				●				
T-66 PRACTICE STORE				●				
5.0" HVAR TARGET ROCKET KIT	●	●	●			●	●	●
AERO 6A PKG. (7 - 2.75" ROCKETS)	●	●	●	●	●	●	●	●
[1] AERO 7D ROCKET PKG	●	●	●	●	●	●	●	●
[2] SIDEWINDER	●	●		●	●		●	●
[3] SPARROW	●	●		●	●		●	●
STARTER UNIT				●				
282 GALLON FUEL TANK				●	●			

[1] DO NOT USE ON AERO 14 TYPE RACK
[2] SIDEWINDER - USE AERO 1A LAUNCHER
[3] SPARROW I - USE AERO 3A LAUNCHER
SPARROW III - USE AERO 4A LAUNCHER

SOURCE - F3H-2 NAVWEPS MANUAL

The full range of stores compatibility at the various hardpoints on the F3H Demon are depicted in the graphic above. (Artwork by Rock Roszak)

LANDING GEAR DETAILS

The nose landing gear on the Demon was a simple design with a single wheel. The gear retracted aft into its well, which was covered by two doors. The three approach lights were in a small box mounted on the main strut. Note that the two side links are not the same. The one on the right side had a bend near the top to provide clearance with the light box as the gear moved through its retraction/extension cycle. (Kinzey)

There were no antennas mounted on the right nose gear door, but it did have the series of vents. The scissors link for the nose gear was a very unusual design. (Kinzey)

Right: The inside surface of the left nose gear door is shown here. Lightening holes were cut into its inner skin. It was hinged at two places, and a link between it and the retraction arm opened and closed the door as the gear cycled. (Kinzey)

Additional details of the nose gear can be seen from the left side. Note how the door hangs clear of the fuselage when open. A series of vents are on the door. The oval-shaped area and small holes just forward of and below the vents indicates the mounting location for the lower UHF blade antenna, although the antenna is not present on this restored aircraft. The circular area at the aft end of the door is where the IFF antenna was located. Again it is not present on this aircraft. (Kinzey)

This is an enlarged, cropped area from the photograph used in the Introduction to this publication. It is included here to show the lower UHF blade antenna and the circular IFF antenna that were usually installed on the left nose gear door on operational Demons. (National Naval Aviation Museum)

60

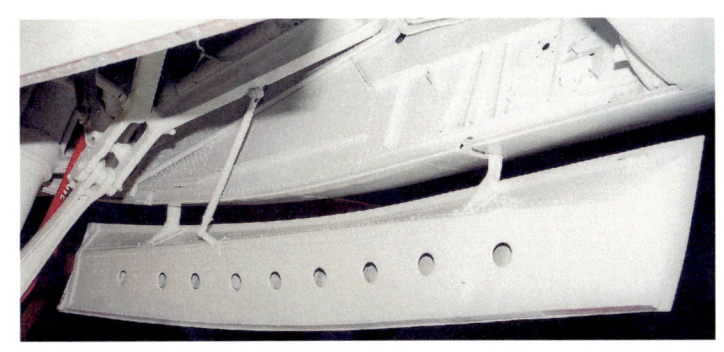

The inside surface of the right nose gear door was basically a mirror image of the left. Again note the link between the door and the retraction arm that opened and closed the door. (Kinzey)

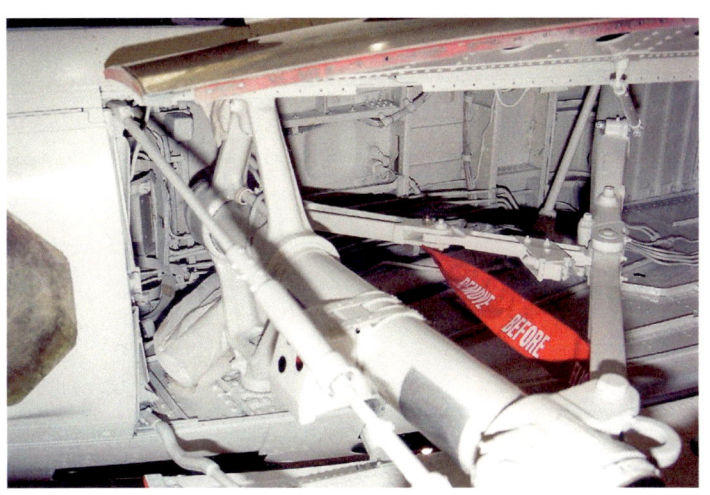

This view looks up in front of the main nose gear strut into the forward end of the nose gear well. Numerous lines and wiring harnesses ran along the top and sides of the well. The "Remove Before Flight" streamer is attached to a pin installed in the retraction linkage to prevent accidental retraction while the aircraft is on the ground. (Kinzey)

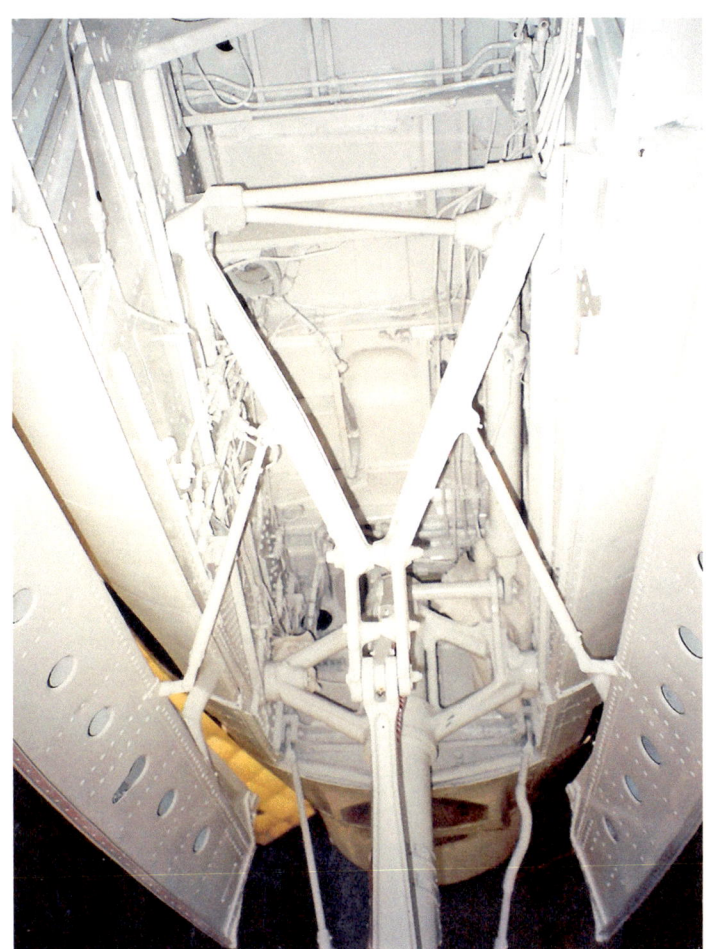

The center section of the nose gear well is shown here, as is the right side wall. (Kinzey)

The forward end of the nose gear well is visible in this view as is most of the Y-shaped linkage that retracted and extended the gear. (Kinzey)

Left: The aft end of the gear well was simpler than the front, but several lines are present. The wheel and tire fit into this area when the gear was retracted. (Kinzey)

An inside front view of the left main gear provides a good look at the details of the wheel and three of the four doors that covered the well when the gear was retracted. Note the tie-down point at the center of the wheel hub. Landing gear doors often had red edges as a safety measure. The retraction link is also shown to good effect from this angle. (Kinzey)

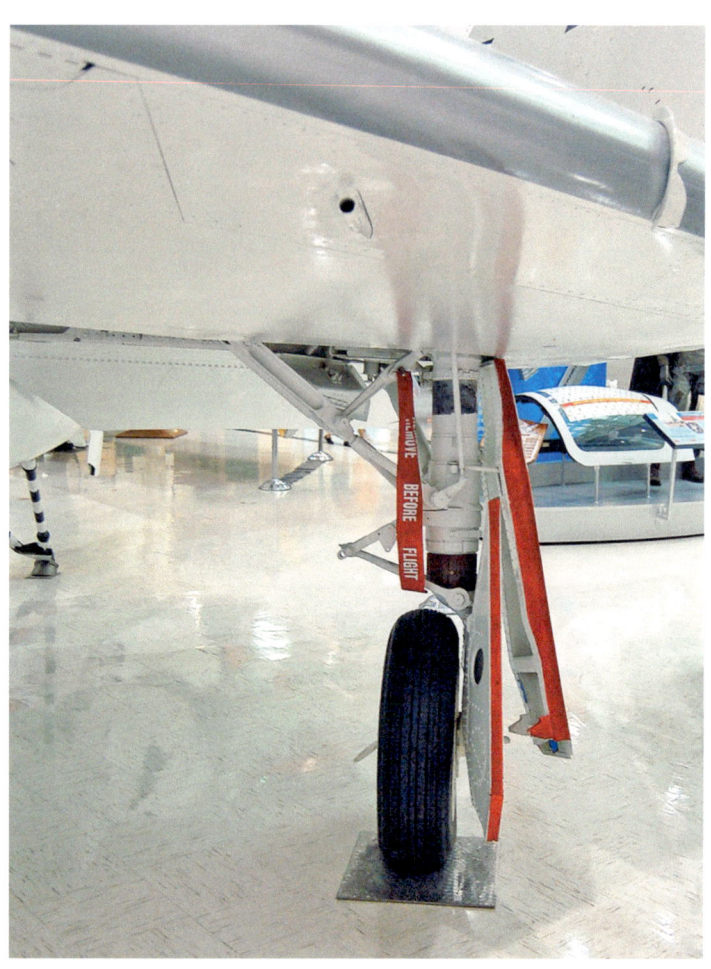

This front view shows the mounting angles for the two doors that were attached to the strut. Smaller links and arms are also visible. (Kinzey)

From behind and slightly outboard of the left landing gear, the rear bracing strut can be seen, as can the scissors link on the oleo portion of the gear. (Kinzey)

Details inside most of the left gear well are revealed in this view. Note the four springs in various locations. A black metal placard with silver lettering was on the upper part of the main strut. (Kinzey)

62

Although the inner gear door is closed on this Demon as displayed at the National Naval Aviation Museum, this photo shows much of the inner part of the well where the wheel and tire would be when the gear was retracted. A photo of this inner part of the well, taken with the door in the open position, can be found in the Demon Restoration chapter in this publication. (Kinzey)

Right: From this angle, the upper-most part of the left gear strut is visible inside the well, as is the rather complex linkage that retracts and extends the gear. (Kinzey)

The right main landing gear was simply a reverse of the left. The safety pin with the "Remove Before Flight" streamer was to insure the gear did not accidentally retract or collapse when the aircraft was on the ground. Note the small linkage arms that held the outer door closed when the gear was retracted. (Kinzey)

From behind the right landing gear, the rear strength brace, retraction linkage, oleo scissors link, and the mounting angles of the doors are visible. (Kinzey)

This excellent front view provides a good look at details of the right landing gear. It should be noted that metal bands are placed over the oleo portion of the museum aircraft to keep the strut from compressing with no hydraulic pressure in the aircraft. The band is the height the oleo would be under normal hydraulic pressure. (Kinzey)

In this outside view of the right main gear, the depth of the wheel can be seen. Details of the hinge for the outer-most door are also visible. (Kinzey)

Additional details of the main gear wheel and the inner of the two outer-most doors are revealed in this photograph taken from outside the right main gear and slightly aft of it. Note that the leading edge of the outer-most door is not straight, but it has a small dogleg near the top. This view also provides a look at the inside surface of the small door that covers the aft bracing strut for the gear. (Kinzey)

Each main gear well contained the structure for mounting the gear to the wing. This had to be strong enough to endure the stresses of arrested recoveries aboard aircraft carriers. It also included the mechanism that cycled the gear and held it in place when retracted. Hydraulic lines also passed through the well. A total of four doors covered each main gear when retracted. (Kinzey)

64

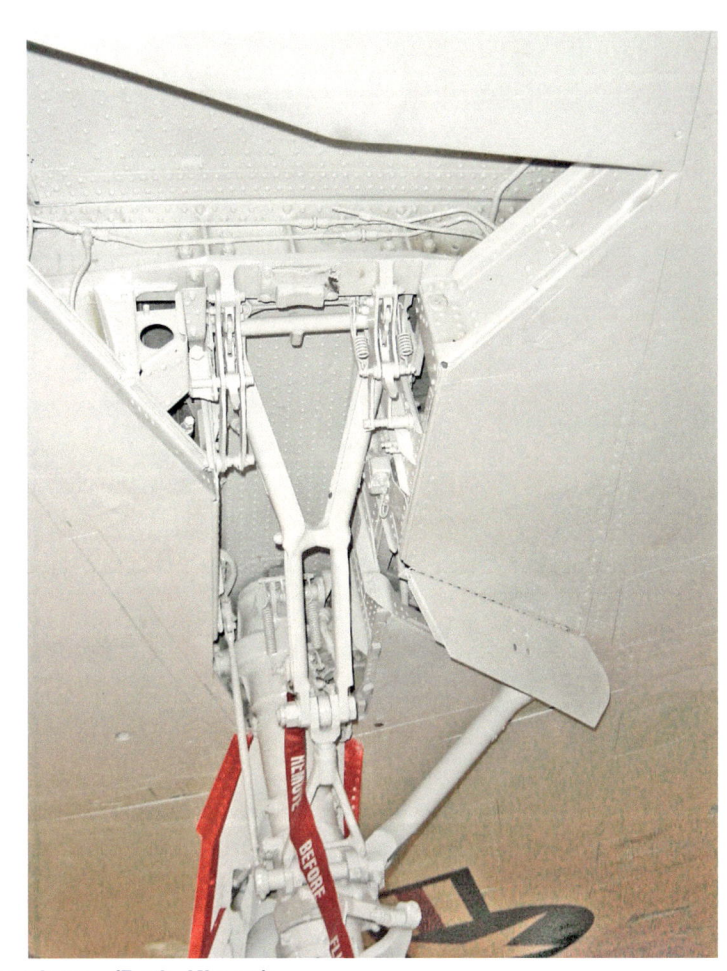

Additional details inside the right gear well are revealed in these views. (Both, Kinzey)

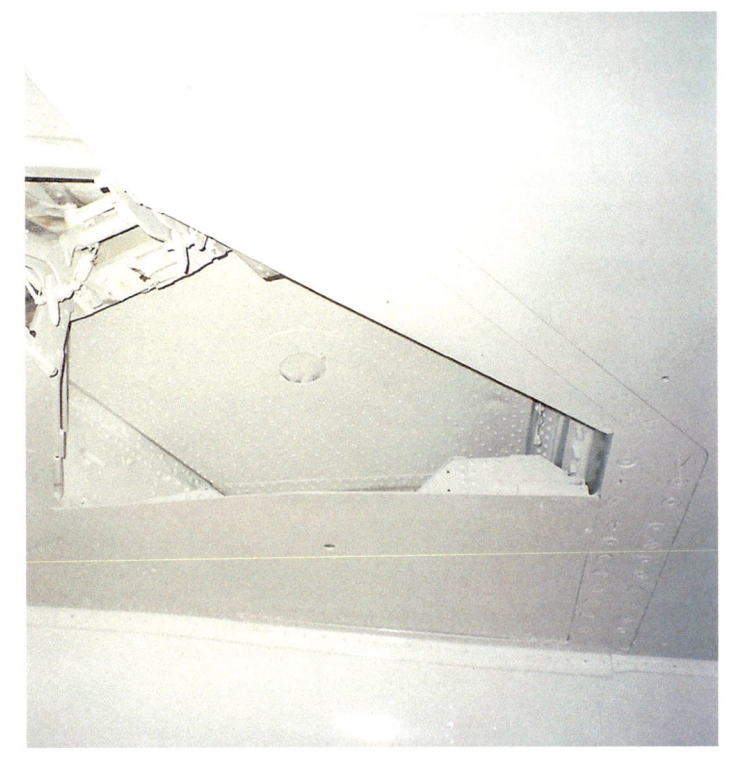

With the inner door in the closed position, it is not possible to see the entire inner area of the well, but much of it is visible. (Kinzey)

Taken during the restoration of the F3H-2M at the National Naval Aviation Museum, this photograph is included in this section, because it shows the large inner gear door for the right landing gear in the open position, as it would be on an operational Demon when the aircraft was on the ground. The rest of the inner portion of the gear well is also visible. This is the same aircraft as in the other photos in this section, only it was taken prior to the completion of the restoration. (Kinzey)

TAIL DETAILS

The Demon had a conventional vertical tail and rudder combination. Depending on aircraft loading and oleo extension, the top of the rudder was approximately fourteen and one half feet above the ground line. Near the end of their operational service, some F3H-2N and F3H-2 Demons had red beacon lights added to the top of their vertical tails. However no F3H-2Ms had the beacon, because all were withdrawn from service prior to its installation. (Kinzey)

The leading edge of the vertical tail was gently curved as it neared the fuselage. Silver Corogard was applied to the leading edge. (Roszak)

The rudder spanned the full height of the vertical tail and was hinged in two places. Unlike some other aircraft delivered in the Light Gull Gray over white paint scheme, contractual specifications did not call for the rudder to be painted white, so it was painted Light Gull Gray as the aircraft left the factory. However, some squadrons elected to paint the rudder white or other colors as is the case here. (Kinzey)

In most cases, the last four digits of the bureau number were painted in large numerals at the base of the vertical tail, even though the complete number was usually stenciled on the aft fuselage below the aircraft's designation. The fin cap on top of the vertical tail housed the upper UHF antenna. (Kinzey)

A small tubular air inlet was located high on the leading edge of the vertical tail. It was the ram air inlet for the artificial feel system for the flight controls. (Kinzey)

Left: Because it housed the upper UHF antenna, the fin cap was made of Fiberglass. The corresponding top of the rudder was also Fiberglass. The fin cap and top of the rudder were often painted in the squadron's color as seen here. (Kinzey)

The Demon was fitted with an all-flying horizontal tail, meaning that the entire surface of the horizontal tails moved to provide pitch control rather than having a combination of a fixed horizontal stabilizer and a movable elevator. The all-flying tail became necessary for positive control as aircraft approached the speed of sound. The combination of the stabilizer and the elevator was called a stabilator. (Kinzey)

Each stabilator was hinged at the center. Two vertical parts of the stabilator covered the hole in the aft fuselage that was necessary for the hinge linkage to move up and down. The upper cover for the hinge opening can be seen here. (Kinzey)

The lower covering for the hole in the fuselage for the left stabilator is shown here. It should be noted that on production aircraft, the natural metal area aft of the engine usually extended all the way to the end of the beaver tail. (Kinzey)

The upper surface of the right stabilator is shown in this view. Note that the leading edge is painted with silver Corogard. The span of the horizontal tail was fifteen feet, eight inches. The stabilators were mounted level with no dihedral or anhedral. The long beaver tail with its flat upper surface, as used on the F3H-2N and F3H-2M, is also visible in this photograph. (Kinzey)

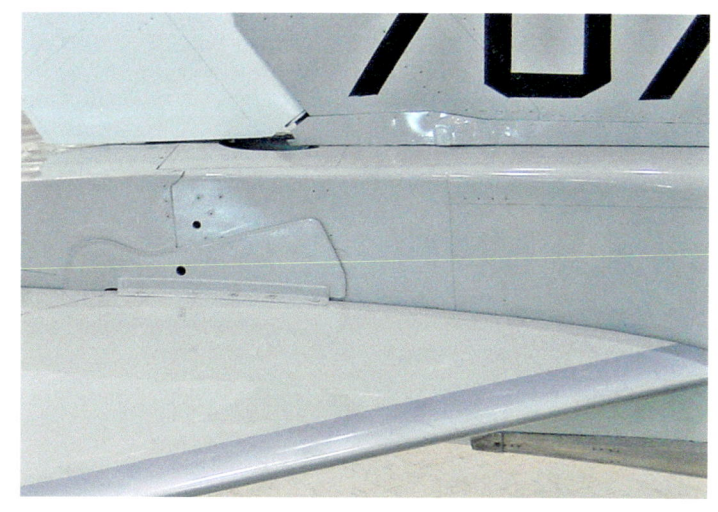

This view shows the underside of the right stabilator. As noted elsewhere in this publication, on operational Demons, the inner half of the underside of each stabilator was usually painted with heat resistant silver enamel. They were not bare metal as later used on the F-4 Phantom II. (Kinzey)

Details of the top hinge plate for the right stabilator are shown in this close-up. (Kinzey)

67

An underside view shows the lower part of the right hinge plate. (Kinzey)

Above and below: The long beaver tail used on the F3H-2N and F3H-2M is shown in these two photographs. It had a flat upper surface, while the short beaver tail had a curved upper surface and was almost two feet shorter in length. (Both, Kinzey)

Whether a Demon had the long or short beaver tail, a white position light was located at the aft end. (Kinzey)

ENGINE DETAILS

This Allison J71 engine is on display at the National Naval Aviation Museum aboard NAS Pensacola, Florida. Areas have been cut away to reveal the inner workings of the powerplant, however the afterburner is not displayed with the basic engine. The only two production aircraft powered by the J71 were the Demon and the B-66 Destroyer, a medium, twin-engine bomber used by the U. S. Air Force. J71s had also been used on the XA3D-1 Skywarrior prototypes, however production A3Ds were powered by Pratt & Whitney J57-P-10 turbojets. (Kinzey)

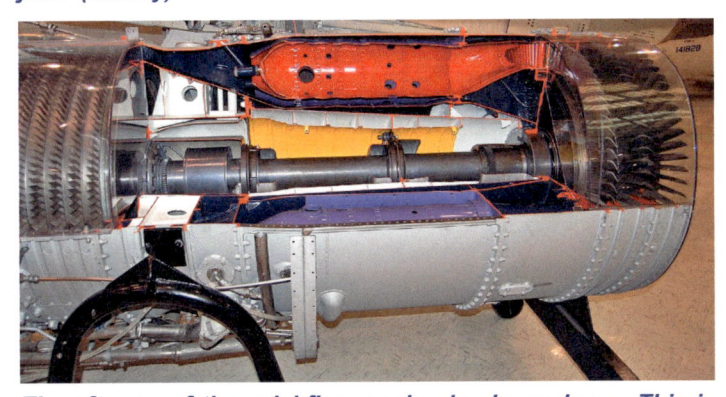

Details on the front of the engine are shown here including the accessories. Note the rows of compressor blades. When it was discovered that very cold damp air could cause the engine shroud to contract around the compressor to the point that it came in contact with the blades, thus causing a flameout, Allison solved the problem by shaving the tips of the blades down to decrease their diameter. This resulted in a significant loss of thrust. (Kinzey)

The aft area of the axial-flow engine is shown here. This is where combustion took place. The engine was just over 287 inches long and about 43 inches in diameter. The J71-A-2B version, used in the F3H-2, was slightly smaller than the J71-A-2 used in the F3H-2N and F3H-2M. See the data information for each Demon variant for exact dimensions. (Kinzey)

A convergent-divergent nozzle was mounted at the aft end of the afterburner. It could be opened or closed to regulate thrust. The nozzle, and the area surrounding it, were unpainted natural metal. (Kinzey)

The convergent-divergent nozzle is shown here from the right side. Photographs indicate that on operational Demons, the natural metal area aft of the nozzle extended all the way to the beaver tail. On the underside of the stabilators, the inner half was painted with a heat-resistant silver enamel on operational Demons. (Roszak)

This view looks forward inside the convergent-divergent nozzle to the flame holder at the other end of the afterburner. Details on the inside of the afterburner are also visible. (Kinzey)

DEMON SQUADRONS GALLERY

An F3H-2N from VF-124 is maneuvered onto Catapult TWO aboard USS LEXINGTON, CVA-16. The "Moonshiners" deployed to the Western Pacific aboard LEX in 1957. (National Naval Aviation Museum)

Between 1956 and 1964, eight fighter squadrons of the Atlantic Fleet and sixteen assigned to the Pacific Fleet flew one or more versions of the Demon. Additionally, one composite training squadron on the west coast also had Demons in its inventory of aircraft. Several test and evaluation units flew the Demon to develop improvements and test weapons, especially the three types of air-to-air missiles used with the aircraft.

The three squadrons that originally received the F3H-2M variant, VF-61, VF-24, and VF-112, flew only that version of the Demon, and they did so for a relatively short period of time before the F3H-2M was withdrawn from service. Other Demon squadrons initially flew the F3H-2N, but as the F3H-2 became operational and F3H-2Ns were upgraded to F3H-2 standards, both versions could be found serving together in the same unit.

The Atlantic Fleet squadrons made eleven deployments to the Mediterranean Sea aboard various carriers, while the Pacific Fleet squadrons deployed on twenty-nine cruises to the Western Pacific. Additionally, Demons from both fleets participated aboard carriers on shake-down cruises and various training exercises as well as conducting numerous short at-sea periods for qualifications.

Demon deployments were made on ESSEX, MIDWAY, and FORRESTAL class carriers. All three MIDWAY class carriers made deployments with Demons in their air wings, as did all four FORRESTAL class supercarriers. But for the ESSEX class carriers, deployments by Demon squadrons were made only aboard those ships that had received the SCB-27C conversion. This conversion included the installation of two steam catapults with large jet blast deflectors (JBDs) aft of them that were capable of withstanding the heat of jet engines equipped with afterburners. These ships retained their attack carrier (CVA) status throughout the 1960s and into the 1970s, long after the Demon had been withdrawn from service. All of these ships had also received the SCB-125 conversion, which included the angled deck and enclosed bow.

None of the Demon deployments were made aboard ESSEX class carriers that had received the SCB-27A conversion. These ships retained their shorter hydraulic catapults rather than being fitted with steam catapults, and they were reclassified as anti-submarine support carriers (CVS) in the late 1950s. The hydraulic catapults could not launch the heavier aircraft that the steam catapults could, and their jet blast deflectors were not capable of withstanding the heat generated by afterburners. It must be noted however, that these ESSEX class ships did have a limited capability to operate the Demon, even with their hydraulic catapults. On at least three occasions, Demons conducted carrier qualifications aboard ESSEX class carriers with hydraulic catapults. VF-114 conducted quals aboard USS HORNET, CVS-12, and a rare color photograph of one of their Demons about to launch from one of that carrier's hydraulic catapults is included in the VF-114 section of this chapter. Another known qualification with Demons aboard an ESSEX class carrier with hydraulic catapults was when VF-112 took its F3H-2Ms aboard USS KEARSARGE, CVA-33. VF-122 also conducted qualifications aboard KEARSARGE.

ATLANTIC FLEET SQUADRONS
VF-13 "Aggressors"

The "Aggressors" of VF-13 received their Demons late in the operational service life of the aircraft, transitioning from F4D-1 Skyrays in September 1962. Its F3H-2s were transferred to the squadron from VF-131, which was decommissioned that same month, and the markings used by both VF-131 and VF-13 were the same. All VF-13 had to do was to paint out the second 1 in VF-131 and change the name of the aircraft carrier painted on the side of VF-131's F3H-2s. Everything else, including the tail codes, remained the same. (Artwork by Rock Roszak)

Two Demons from VF-13 fly together in 1963. By this time, the F3H-2 had been redesignated F-3B. Number 104 carries a Sparrow III missile on its right outboard pylon, and both aircraft have one 282-gallon fuel tank on a fuselage station. The assignment of the squadron to USS SHANGRI-LA, CVA-38, is painted on the fuselage of each aircraft. These two F-3Bs have the beacon added to the fin cap on the vertical tail, a feature seen on many Demons late in their operational life. (National Naval Aviation Museum)

F-3B, BuNo. 143492, is shown being loaded onto USS SHANGRI-LA, at Mayport, Florida. This aircraft has all four types of pylons usually associated with the Demon installed under its wings and fuselage. One of the large pylons is attached to the left fuselage station, and it has a 282-gallon fuel tank loaded on it. The right outboard station has a pylon with an AERO 4A launcher for the Sparrow III missile, and the inboard pylon has an AERO 1A launcher used with the Sidewinder missile. Between them on the center wing station is an AERO 24 pylon used with rocket pods and bombs weighing up to 500 pounds. Note that the upper 20-mm cannon has been removed and its gun port faired over. Also evident in this view is the long oleo portion of the nose strut. (National Naval Aviation Museum)

VF-14 "Top Hatters"

The "Top Hatters" of VF-14 were, and remain to this day, a squadron of firsts. In fact, they were the Navy's very first fighter squadron, originally formed in 1919, although it was not designated VF-14 at that time. They became the first fleet squadron to transition to the Demon when they traded in their F3D Skyknights for F3H-2Ns in March 1956. VF-14 would make four cruises to the Mediterranean as part of CVG-1, and all would be made aboard USS FRANKLIN D. ROOSEVELT, CVA-42. The tail code for all four cruises was AB, and the "Top Hatters" applied their well-known red fuselage flash with the white disc and black top hat to their Demons. (Artwork by Rock Roszak)

71

This overhead view shows one of VF-14's F3H-2Ns on the Elevator ONE aboard USS FORRESTAL, CVA-59. It has the T tail code used by CVG-1 for that cruise, and the stripes are red. Note that this early F3H-2N does not have the wing spoilers nor the in-flight refueling probe. (National Naval Aviation Museum)

An F3H-2 from VF-14 is hooked up to Cat ONE aboard USS FRANKLIN D. ROOSEVELT, CVA-42, in June 1961. A captive training version of the Sidewinder missile is loaded on station one. Note that the upper 20-mm cannons have been deleted and their gun ports faired over. (National Naval Aviation Museum)

VF-31 "Tomcatters"

F3H-2, BuNo. 143450, passes over the wires as it recovers aboard USS SARATOGA, CVA-60. Markings used by VF-31 on its Demons changed several times, and these included Felix kicking up stars as he ran with his bomb on the sides of the fuselage. The red fin cap is a pennant style rather than being a solid red cap. (National Naval Aviation Museum)

Right: Markings used by VF-31 for their first cruise aboard USS SARATOGA, CVA-60, included a red flash on the fuselage and red bands on the tail with the AC tail code in black, outlined in white. The fin cap was red and was the pennant style rather then being solid red. The unit's insignia, consisting of Felix the Cat with his bomb on a yellow disc, was painted just below the fin cap on the vertical tail. VF 31 was lettered in black on each speed brake. BuNo. 136992 was one of thirty F3H-2Ns in production block h. During this cruise, VF-31 participated in a show of strength during the crisis in Lebanon. (National Naval Aviation Museum)

McDonnell F3H-2 *DEMON*

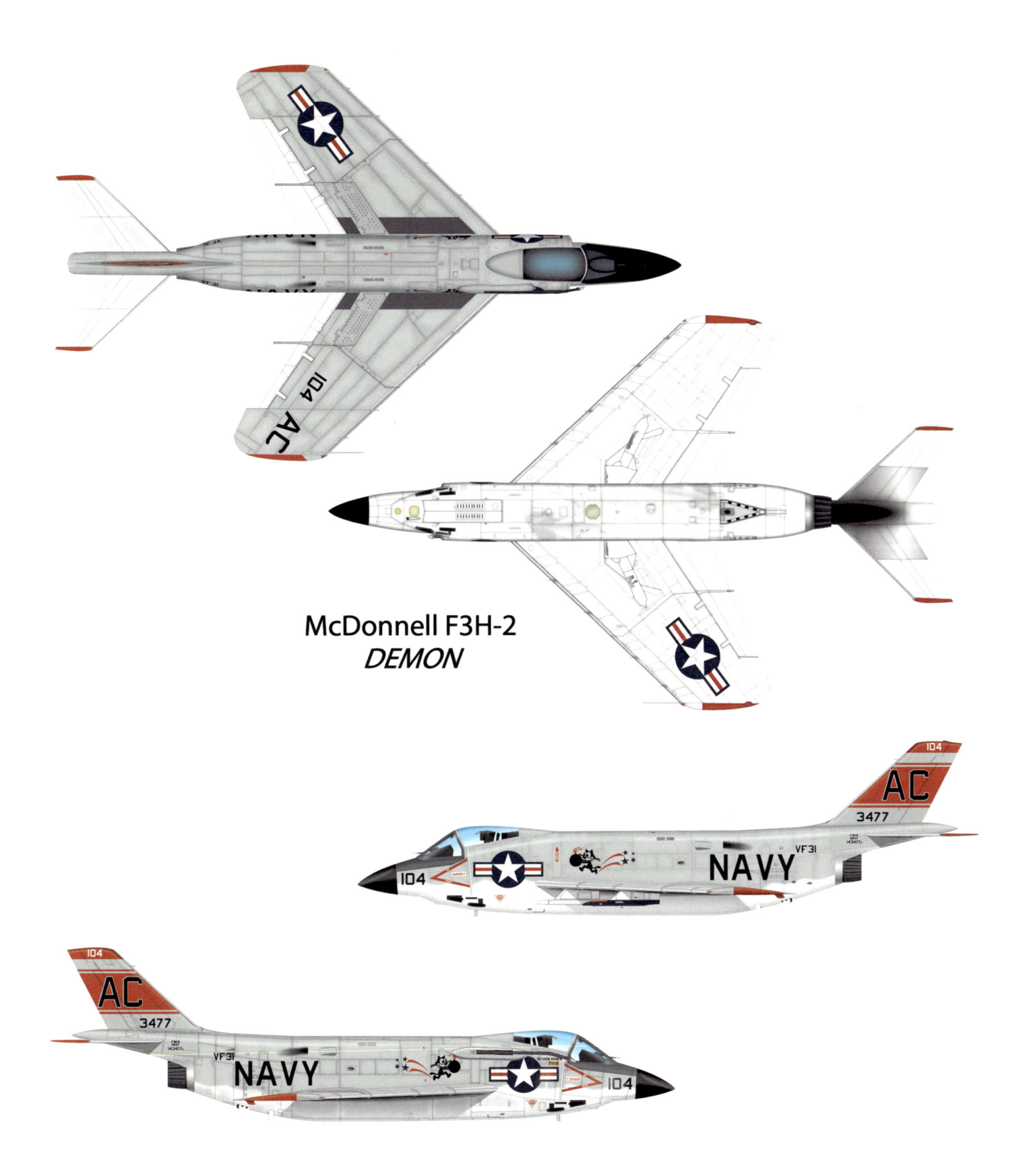

VF-31, with its famous "Felix the Cat" insignia, traces it lineage and history back to Grumman FF-1 biplanes. Its use of Demons began in 1956 when it transitioned from F2H Banshees to F3H-2Ns at Cecil Field, Florida. Initially, the squadron was assigned a K tail code, but by the time it made its first of five deployments with the Demon as part of CVG-3 aboard USS SARATOGA, CVA-60, it had changed to AC for its tail code. (Artwork by Rock Roszak)

73

VF-31 started receiving F3H-2s as soon as they became available. Here, BuNo. 143477, is seen with Felix the Cat painted prominently on each side of the fuselage with red flashes and dark blue stars. Note that the entire fin cap is painted red rather than having the pennant style red marking as seen in the photo of the F3H-2 landing aboard SARATOGA previously. This aircraft is the subject of our four-view artwork. (National Naval Aviation Museum)

The squadron commander's F3H-2 displays the markings used by VF-31 in 1962 and 1963. A large red chevron is on each side of the fuselage, and the Felix the Cat insignia with its yellow disc is at the angle. There is no color on the fin cap, and most of the rudder on this aircraft is painted white. VF-31 is painted above the N in NAVY on the fuselage. Note the unusual treatment of the jet intake warning chevron in front of the inlet. DANGER JET INTAKE is lettered in white on both parts of the chevron rather than having DANGER in red on a white rectangle. (National Naval Aviation Museum)

VF-41 "Black Aces"

Markings used by VF-41 for most of the time the "Black Aces" flew Demons are shown on F3H-2, BuNo. 143449. The squadron made two deployments aboard USS INDEPENDENCE, CVA-62, as part of CVG-7, while equipped with F3H-2s. (National Naval Aviation Museum)

An F9F-8 Cougar taxis in front of VF-41 Demons on the wooden flight deck of USS INTREPID, CVA-11, in October 1958. The aircraft were part of ATG-181, and the markings used on the "Black Aces" F3H-2s are visible in this photograph. Red and black stripes are on the vertical tail, and the squadron's insignia is painted in a red band, outlined in black, on the sides of fuselage. ATG-181 used AM as its tail code. (Photo courtesy of Bill Chaney)

74

VF-61 "Jolly Rogers"

An F3H-2M assigned to VF-61 is positioned on the starboard elevator aboard USS FRANKLIN D. ROOSEVELT, CVA-42, in April 1957. At that time the squadron used E as their tail code as part of CVG-8, and the only unit markings were the black and white flag on the fuselage and VF-61 above the speed brake. (National Naval Aviation Museum)

Two of VF-61s F3H-2Ms are seen on the flight deck of USS FRANKLIN D. ROOSEVELT, as aircraft are respotted. Note that the aircraft at the right has the addition of the black rudder with eight yellow diamonds as part of the unit's markings. A yellow band with a thin black outline would later be added above the tail code. (National Naval Aviation Museum)

The "Jolly Rogers" started using the AG tail code in 1957. The aft end of the canopy was painted yellow, and small black triangles were painted around its edge. The wing tips and the tips of the horizontal stabilators were painted black with yellow diamonds. 203 is shown here on Cat FOUR aboard USS SARATOGA, CVA-60. In 1958, the AG tail code was changed to AJ, but all other markings stayed the same. (National Naval Aviation Museum)

VF-82 "Iron Men"

The "Iron Men" of VF-82 flew F3H-2 Demons briefly between 1956 and early 1959. Both VF-61 and VF-82 were assigned to CVG-8, and the "Iron Men's" markings were the same as those used by the "Jolly Rogers" while flying Demons, only the colors for VF-82 were red and white rather than yellow and black. These included a white rudder with red diamonds, and white wing tips, also with red diamonds, that wrapped around the tip. A red tail band, bordered in white was above the tail code. The tail code was originally E, but it was later changed to AJ, the same as the last code for VF-61. Both VF-61 and VF-82 were decommissioned on the same day, April 15, 1959, at NAS Oceana, Virginia. (Artwork by Rock Roszak)

F3H-2, BuNo. 143450, displays the markings used by VF-82, during the squadron's relatively brief time in Demons. The photograph is dated May 1958, and was taken aboard USS FORRESTAL, CVA-59. CVG-8's AJ tail code replaced the earlier E used by the unit. (National Naval Aviation Museum)

VF-101 "Grim Reapers"

In April of 1958, VF-101 moved from NAS Cecil Field to NAS Key West, Florida, to become the training squadron for the Atlantic Fleet for both F4D-1 Skyray and F3H Demon fighters. From 1958 until 1962, the "Grim Reapers" had F3H-2s in their mixed inventory. Their markings included an AD tail code and a red band with white stars just below the fin cap on the vertical tail. On most Demons, the wing tips were also painted red. VF 101 (with no dash) was painted on each side of the fuselage above the wing. (Artwork by Rock Roszak)

An F3H-2 from VF-101 taxies forward with wings folded on the flight deck of USS INTREPID, CVA-11, during carrier qualifications in April 1960. Note the red wing tips. The red band with the white stars on the vertical tail and the AD tail code are difficult to see from this angle, but they are discernable. (National Naval Aviation Museum)

76

VF-131 "Nightcappers"

This VF-131 Demon was one of the F3H-2s assigned to the "Nightcappers." Unlike VF-131's Demons shown in some of the other photos of this section, this one has the squadron's insignia painted within the fuselage band. Some squadrons left out the dash when painting their designations on the aircraft, and VF-131 was a unit that followed this practice. (Artwork by Rock Roszak)

An F3H-2 assigned to VF-131 is shown aboard USS INDEPENDENCE, CVA-62, when the "Nightcappers" conducted carrier qualifications aboard that carrier while USS CONSTELLATION, CVA-64, was still fitting out. Note that USS CONSTELLATION is lettered on the side of the fuselage in anticipation of the squadron being assigned to CVA-64. There are no squadron or air wing markings on the vertical tail other than the AE tail code. (Photo from the collection of Don Spering)

BuNo. 133572, was also an F3H-2N that was upgraded to F3H-2 standards and assigned to VF-131. This is one of the few examples where the short beaver tail replaced the original longer version on an upgraded aircraft. This could have been a replacement for a longer tail that had been damaged, because this change was not normally a part of the upgrade. The designation on the fuselage also indicates F3H-2, but many upgraded F3H-2Ns still carried their original designation above the full bureau number on the aft fuselage. (National Naval Aviation Museum)

The squadron commander's Demon is shown here at NAS Cecil Field in 1962. This was one of the F3H-2Ns, BuNo. 136996, that was upgraded to F3H-2 standards. Note that the aircraft retains its original long beaver tail. AERO 4A launch rails for Sparrow III missiles are loaded on the outboard pylons, while AERO 1A launchers for Sidewinders are on the inboard wing pylons. Only the two lower 20-mm cannons are retained. The intake warning chevron has DANGER JET INTAKE lettered on both the upper and lower segments, rather than having the word DANGER in red on a white rectangle within the chevron as was the more common practice. (National Naval Aviation Museum)

This VF-131 Demon, BuNo. 143487, was one of the F3H-2s assigned to the "Nightcappers." Unlike VF-131's Demons shown in the other photos of this section, this one has the squadron's insignia painted within the fuselage band. Some squadrons left out the dash when painting their designations on the aircraft, and VF-131 was a unit that followed this practice. (National Naval Aviation Museum)

PACIFIC FLEET SQUADRONS
VC-3 and VF(AW)-3

Composite Squadron THREE (VC-3) was assigned the mission of training replacement pilots, aircrew, and maintenance personnel for fleet squadrons. VF(AW)-3 was another squadron that was involved with training, focusing on aircraft that were designed to fight in an all-weather environment. They also worked in coordination with the U. S. Air Force's air defense forces, supplementing them with F4D-1 Skyrays. On July 1, 1956, VC-3 and VF(AW)-3 merged, continuing their training roles as a single unit. Their Demons were simply marked with an NP tail code, and a blue band with white stars was added just below the fin cap. (Artwork by Rock Roszak)

F3H-2N, BuNo. 133582, was one of the Demons assigned to VF(AW)-3 after the merger with VC-3. The tail code is NP, and a blue band with white stars is just below the fin cap. Note the unusual treatment of the white rectangle with the word DANGER in red that is associated with the jet intake chevron. Usually, this marking would be inside the chevron, but it is forward of it and is partially painted over by the second 1 in the modex. Also note that the inside half on the underside of the horizontal stabilizer is painted with the heat resistant silver enamel. (Photo from the collection of Lloyd Jones)

VF-21 "Freelancers"

VF-21 was a redesignation of VF-64 that took place on July 1, 1959, at NAS Alameda, California. At that time, VF-64 was already flying Demons and was assigned to the air wing aboard USS MIDWAY, CVA-41. Under their new designation, and with their new name, "Freelancers," the squadron remained assigned to CVG-2 aboard MIDWAY. The NE tail code was used by the air group for all three cruises. The squadron insignia was displayed on a black flash on the fuselage, and yellow tips were painted on vertical tail, wings, and stabilators, with three yellow stripes on the rudder. (Artwork by Rock Roszak)

This is the same F3H-2, BuNo. 143435, shown in the profile above. It has made an emergency landing aboard USS MIDWAY, taking the barrier in the process. Note the various responsibilities of the flight deck crew as they respond to the emergency. Several are bringing a ladder to the aircraft to permit the pilot to egress quickly. Other teams are standing by with fire-fighting apparatus in the event of a fire, while others scramble to remove the aircraft from the barrier so that flight operations can resume quickly. Fortunately, there appears to be little damage to the Demon. (National Naval Aviation Museum)

VF-24 "Corsairs"

VF-24 was one of only three Navy fleet squadrons to fly the F3H-2M version of the Demon. Their transition from the FJ-3 Fury to the F3H-2M began in 1957, at NAS Moffett Field, California. Initially, their markings included an NE tail code as part of CVG-2. After reassignment to CVG-21, the "Corsairs" made their only deployment while flying Demons, a cruise aboard USS LEXINGTON, CVA-16. While assigned to CVG-21, the squadron used NP as their tail code. (Artwork by Rock Roszak)

F3H-2M, BuNo. 137088, is shown shortly after VF-24 received its Demons and while the "Corsairs" were assigned to CVG-2 and used the NE tail code. Note that the last four digits of the Bureau number are not displayed at the base of the vertical tail in large numerals as was usually done on Demons. The distinctive fuselage flash, used later by VF-24, is also not displayed on this aircraft. A color photograph of another F3H-2M assigned to VF-24, and showing the unit's later markings and tail code, can be found in the F3H-2M section of the Demon Variants chapter. (National Naval Aviation Museum)

VF-53 "Blue Knights"

Above: VF-53 was established at NAS Alameda, California, in 1958 as a redesignation of VF-123. It also received its first F3H-2 Demons at that time. Throughout the three years they flew Demons, they remained a part of CVG-5 and used NF as their tail code. Interestingly, except for the VF-53 painted on the aft fuselage below NAVY, the unit did not use any distinctive markings on their aircraft. (Artwork by Rock Roszak)

Left: The complete lack of distinctive markings on VF-53's Demons is illustrated by this photograph of F3H-2, BuNo. 145303. The only marking that identifies this aircraft as belonging to the "Blue Knights" is the VF-53 on the aft fuselage that is applied partially to the speed brake. (National Museum of Naval Aviation)

79

VF-64 "Freelancers"

VF-64 flew Demons for a short period of time in 1958 and 1959. The squadron was assigned to CVG-2 aboard USS MIDWAY, CVA-41, but on July 1, 1959, the unit was redesignated VF-21. The profile above shows an earlier treatment of the squadron insignia, a prancing panther, on the fuselage without the circular logo accompanying it. Also note the more extensive yellow striping on the vertical tail than would be used later by VF-21. (Artwork by Rock Roszak)

One of VF-64's F3H-2s refuels from an AJ-2 Savage tanker. The Demon retains all four of its 20-mm cannons and carries Sidewinders on its inboard wing pylons and Sparrow III missiles on its outboard wing pylons. The aircraft displays the circular squadron insignia on the black flash that would be retained by VF-21, and the less extensive tail striping. (National Naval Aviation Museum)

VF-92 and VF-54 "Silver Kings"

The "Silver Kings" had the unique distinction of flying F3H-2N and F3H-2 Demons under two squadron designations, using VF-92 twice. In May 1959, VF-92 transitioned from F2H-3 Banshees to the F3H Demon as part of CVG-9 (tail code NG) assigned to USS RANGER, CVA-61. Their initial unit markings were nothing more than VF-92 lettered on the side of the fuselage and a yellow fin cap. (Artwork by Rock Roszak)

On June 1, 1962, the squadron was reassigned to CVG-5 and USS TICONDEROGA, CVA-14, and their designation was changed to VF-54. The tail code was also changed from NG to NF. While the unit continued to use minimal squadron markings on their Demons, they increased the size of the yellow at the top of the vertical tail, added a black outline at the bottom, and painted four silver king chess pieces in the yellow area. (Artwork by Rock Roszak)

80

Two of the "Silver Kings'" F3H-2s fly in formation during the time the squadron was redesignated VF-54 and assigned to CVG-5 aboard USS TICONDEROGA, CVA-14. Note the yellow fin cap with the four king pieces as used in the game of chess. (National Naval Aviation Museum)

Although it has the early yellow fin cap used by VF-92, the fact that this Demon has the NF tail code and VF-92 lettered on the fuselage indicates that the photo was taken after the squadron reverted back to the VF-92 designation. This would be very late during the time the "Silver Kings" flew Demons. Also, this F3H-2N has been upgraded to F3H-2 standards to employ the Sparrow III missile, and it is fitted with the Martin Baker H5 ejection seat. (National Naval Aviation Museum)

VF-112

VF-112 began its transition from F9F-8B Cougars to F3H-2M Demons on April 5, 1957, and they would be one of only two Pacific Fleet squadrons to fly the F3H-2M variant of the Demon. Initially their markings included red flashes on the fuselage and vertical tail. (Artwork by Rock Roszak)

VF-112's F3H-2Ms are lined up on the ramp at NAS Miramar, California, shortly after the squadron transitioned to Demons in April 1957. (National Naval Aviation Museum)

Above: Two F3H-2Ms from VF-112 are ready for a formation take off. This photo shows the red flashes on the fuselage and vertical tail used by VF-112 for most of the time it flew Demons. (National Naval Aviation Museum)

Three F3H-2Ms from VF-112 head to the range to conduct a practice firing of Sparrow I missiles. (National Naval Aviation Museum)

VF-112 made one cruise aboard USS TICONDEROGA, CVA-14, as part of ATG-1. For this cruise, the squadron changed its markings. The red flashes on the fuselage and vertical tail were removed, and a white shooting star with a red "1" and a red outline was painted on the fuselage. This marking signified assignment to ATG-1, and it was painted on the other types of aircraft in the group, only each squadron's color was used for the outline and the "1." On the Demons, a small red flash was painted at the top of the vertical tail. Five small red stars were painted on the vertical tail below the fin cap. (Artwork by Rock Roszak)

These two photos were taken aboard USS TICONDEROGA, CVA-14, during VF-112's only deployment with Demons. At left, one of the squadron's F3H-2Ms is spotted forward on the flight deck along with FJ-4B Furies of VA-151. Since the wings on the Demon are folded, it is difficult to see the shooting star on the fuselage, but just enough of it is visible to verify that the outline and "1" on the star were painted in red, which was VF-112's squadron color. Blue is used on the Furies, because VA-151's squadron color was blue. The F3H-2M in the foreground of the photo at the right does not have any unit markings, but the other two are painted in the markings that VF-112 used while on the cruise. Although they are difficult to see in this photo, they consisted of a white shooting star with a red outline and a red "1." There was also a small red flash on the fin cap. (Both, National Naval Aviation Museum)

VF-114 "Executioners"

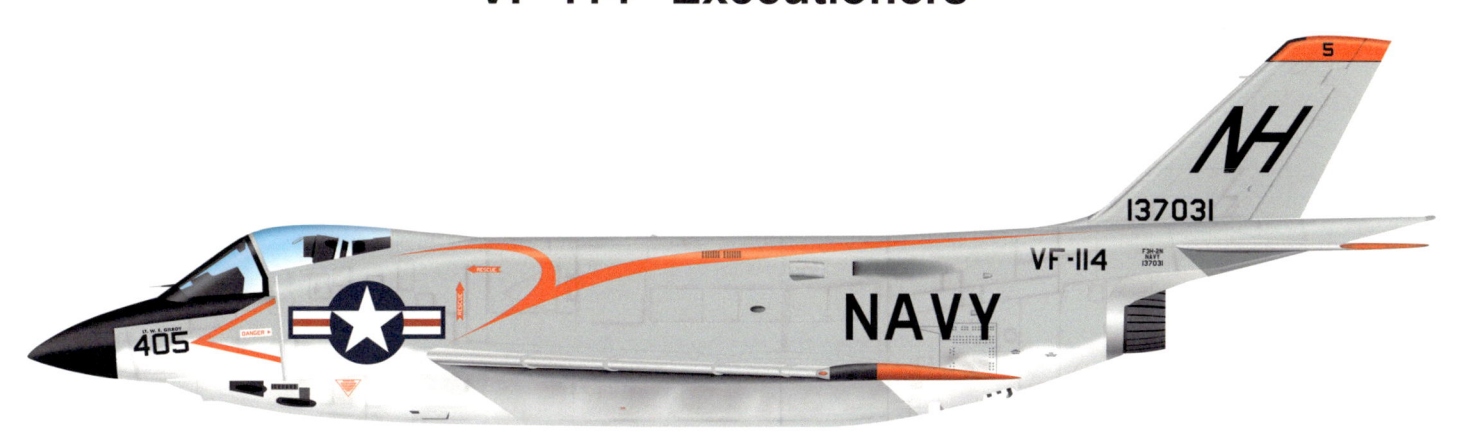

Above: Markings used by VF-114 on their Demons were quite simple yet attractive, featuring a red fuselage flash and a red fin cap on the vertical tail. Throughout their four years flying the Demon, they used the NH tail code as part of CVG-11. (Artwork by Rock Roszak)

Left: An F3H-2N from VF-114 is spotted aft on the starboard side of the flight deck aboard USS SHANGRI-LA, CVA-38, during the "Executioner's" cruise in 1958. BuNo. 137032, was the last F3H-2N produced. (National Naval Aviation Museum)

This rare color photograph shows an F3H-2N from VF-114 that was taken when the "Executioners" were conducting carrier qualifications aboard USS HORNET, CVA-12. This was one of the very few instances when Demons operated aboard ESSEX class carriers that did not have steam catapults. HORNET, and other ESSEX class carriers with hydraulic catapults, were relegated to the anti-submarine support (CVS) role by 1959, leaving only those ESSEX class carriers with steam catapults still operating as attack carriers into the 1960s. (National Naval Aviation Museum)

VF-121 "Pacemakers"

In 1958, VF-121 became the replacement squadron for the Pacific Fleet, flying several types of jet fighters including the F2H Banshee, F11F-1 Tiger, F3D Skyray, and the F3H Demon. The "Pacemakers" mission was to train pilots and maintenance personnel on these aircraft, then send them to operational fleet squadrons. Since they were used in a training role, their aircraft were usually painted with a considerable amount of high-visibility markings. As part of Replacement Air Group 12, they used NJ as their tail code. (Artwork by Rock Roszak)

This low angle view of an F3H-2N assigned to VF-121 provides a good look at the high-visibility areas of the forward fuselage. Note that this aircraft does not have high-visibility areas on the wings. (National Naval Aviation Museum)

F3H-2N, BuNo. 133573, displays the markings carried by VF-121's Demons. Additionally, it has a yellow lightning bolt and a black panther painted on the sides of the aft fuselage. This marking was not on other Demons assigned to the "Pacemakers." Note also that this aircraft has high-visibility panels on the wings. Most of VF-121's Demons did not have high-visibility paint applied to the wings. (National Naval Aviation Museum)

Training for pilots preparing for assignments to fleet squadrons included conducting carrier qualifications. Here an F3H-2 from VF-121 recovers aboard USS ORISKANY, CVA-34, while conducting carrier qualifications. (National Naval Aviation Museum)

This photograph shows the high-visibility markings applied to the tail and aft fuselage of this Demon. Note that this includes the outer portion of each stabilator, and that the high-visibility paint extends all the way to the tip of the beaver tail. However, it should be noted that where the high-visibility paint was applied varied from one aircraft to another. (National Naval Aviation Museum)

VF-122 "Black Angels"

Above: VF-122 began their transition from the F9F-8 Cougar to the F3H-2N Demon in late 1956. The unit's one deployment with the Demon began aboard TICONDEROGA on September 16, 1957, as part of CVG-9. During this cruise, the "Black Angels'" Demons had a black disc with a reddish-orange "9" painted on the fuselage. Three reddish-orange flashes extended aft from the disc. This marking indicated assignment to CVG-9. The tail code was NG, and most aircraft had a reddish-orange band on the vertical tail with a smaller reddish-orange and white trim stripe above and below the band. (Artwork by Rock Roszak)

Left: One of VF-122's F3H-2Ns is launched from the port catapult aboard USS TICONDEROGA, CVA-14, during the squadron's deployment to the Western Pacific as part of Carrier Air Group NINE. Note that this Demon does not have the usual tail markings as seen on the artwork above, VF-122 is painted high on the aft fuselage. (National Naval Aviation Museum)

VF-124 "Moonshiners"

Markings used by VF-124 on its Demons are displayed on this F3H-2N. They consisted of a yellow fuselage flash with a thin black outline. A tall yellow band with two black stripes was painted on the vertical tail, and the single-letter D tail code was used. VF-124 was lettered in black on the aft fuselage. (National Naval Aviation Museum)

An F3H-2N from VF-124 launches from the starboard catapult aboard USS LEXINGTON, CVA-16, in 1958. It has been reported in another publication that the "Moonshiners" did not use the in-flight refueling probe during this deployment, but this photograph clearly shows the probe in place. (National Naval Aviation Museum)

An F3H-2N assigned to VF-124 is brought to a stop after recovering aboard USS LEXINGTON, CVA-16, during carrier qualifications in 1956. Based on the smudges around the gun ports, it appears this Demon has also been doing some gunnery practice. (National Naval Aviation Museum)

VF-141 "Iron Angels"

Markings used by VF-141 were as simple and austere as any used on Demons by fleet squadrons. The squadron's color, red, was applied to the fin cap and it was bordered with a thin black outline. VF-141 was stenciled high on the aft fuselage. No other squadron marking was used. The "Iron Angels" were assigned to Carrier Air Group FOURTEEN, and used that group's NK tail code. F3H-2N, BuNo. 133594, is shown here in June 1961 at NAS Miramar after it had been upgraded to F3H-2 standards. (National Naval Aviation Museum)

An F3H-2 from VF-141 is prepared for launch from the port catapult aboard USS LEXINGTON, CVA-16, in October 1961, during the second WESTPAC cruise for the "Iron Angels" while the squadron flew Demons. Though difficult to see, there is a small white E on a black background, painted on the side of the fuselage just aft of the wing leading edge, indicating that the squadron won the Battle Efficiency "E" award for that year. Note that this aircraft is operating without the detachable refueling probe. (National Naval Aviation Museum)

VF-151 "Vigilantes"

The "Vigilantes" used simple markings for all four years the unit flew Demons, but small changes were made along the way. Initially, the only squadron marking was VF-151 painted high on the aft fuselage. A block style NL tail code was used. By 1960, the fin cap was painted red, which was the squadron's color, and soon after the tail code changed to a slanted style of lettering. The next change was to a red band below the fin cap, and three white silhouettes of a skull clutching a dagger in its teeth were added to the red band. USS CORAL SEA was stenciled in black on the vertical tail. The final change in markings was the addition of three red stripes on a white rudder that appeared in 1963. (Artwork by Rock Roszak)

Although the F3H-2 in the foreground still has the block style NL tail code, the two aircraft in the background to the left have the slanted style of lettering. (National Naval Aviation Museum)

The next change in markings for VF-151 involved replacing the red fin cap with a red band high on the vertical tail. Three white silhouettes of a skull clutching a dagger in its teeth were painted on the red band. USS CORAL SEA was stenciled on the vertical tail just above the last four digits of the bureau number. This F3H-2 has had its upper two 20-mm cannons removed. An AERO 1A launcher for the Sidewinder missile is on the inboard wing pylon, and an AERO 4A launch rail is on the outboard pylon. Also note the addition of the red rotating beacon on top of the fin cap. (National Naval Aviation Museum)

VF-161 "Chargers"

This side view provides a good look at the markings used by the "Chargers" for the entire time the unit flew Demons. It should be noted that the demarcation line between the Light Gull Gray and the white on the fuselage varied considerably on Demons. Some were wavy as shown here, while others were nearly straight. (National Naval Aviation Museum)

87

It's difficult to decide whether to place VF-161 in the Atlantic or Pacific Fleet. Recommissioned at NAS Cecil Field, Florida, on September 1, 1960, the squadron was assigned to Carrier Air Group SIXTEEN. CAG-16 used AH as its tail code, and this Atlantic Fleet designation remained with the group and VF-161 after they were transferred to NAS Miramar, California, for duty with the Pacific Fleet. The squadron would remain at NAS Miramar flying F3H-2Ns and F3H-2s, and they were the last squadron to fly Demons, however they retained their AH tail code the entire time. Because most of their time in Demons was spent based at Miramar NAS, and because both of their deployments were to the Western Pacific, we have chosen to put them with the Pacific Fleet squadrons.

The F-3B assigned to Lt. Dud Farrell sits on the ramp at NAS Miramar near the end of the Demon's operational service. Interestingly, the jet intake warning chevron has no stenciling on it. (National Naval Aviation Museum)

F-3B, BuNo. 146722, is positioned on the starboard catapult aboard USS ORISKANY, CVA-34, during one of the "Chargers" two deployments aboard the carrier to the Western Pacific. Note that the unit's insignia is painted on the fuselage just forward of the red flash. (National Naval Aviation Museum)

VF-193 "Ghost Riders"

This artwork shows the final markings used by VF-193 on its Demons. They consisted of blue flashes painted on the fuselage and tail. Some of the aircraft painted with these markings also had blue wing tips, but photographs show that this one did not. This is the marking scheme displayed on the beautifully restored Demon at the National Naval aviation Museum. (Artwork by Rock Roszak)

A flight of four F3H-2s shows the initial markings applied to VF-193's Demons. These consisted of a medium blue fuselage flash and a matching blue diamond on the vertical tail. Both had a thin white outline. (National Naval Aviation Museum)

Simpler markings used by VF-193 are displayed on F3H-2, BuNo. 145231, as it is prepared for launch from USS BON-HOMME RICHARD, CVA-31. The squadron's markings at this time consist only of a blue fin cap and VF-193 on the aft fuselage. (National Naval Aviation Museum)

This photograph of F3H-2, BuNo. 143440, provides a good look at the initial markings used on VF-193's Demons. The medium blue fuselage flash and diamond on the tail are clearly visible along with the white outline for each. The NM tail code is also outlined in white. Note the low placement of the modex on the nose. There is a small silhouette of what appears to be an F11F-1 Tiger above the national insignia, possibly indicating a practice "kill" over an aircraft from another squadron. LCDR E. I. WHIT-LOCK is stenciled high on the inlet. Both the aircraft silhouette and the pilot's name would be covered with the installation of the in-flight refueling probe. This photo was taken in May 1958 before it became a fairly common practice to delete two or all four of the cannons on F3H-2s. (National Naval Aviation Museum)

VF-213 "Blacklions"

The "Blacklions" of VF-213 transitioned from the F4D Skyray to the F3H Demon in December 1959. Throughout their time with Demons, the squadron's markings remained basically unchanged. They included a prancing black lion on each side of the fuselage and a light blue fin cap with four gold stars. Their Demons always carried an NP tail code, and a 3XX modex was assigned. (Artwork by Rock Roszak)

An in-flight photograph of F3H-2, BuNo. 143471, reveals the name LTJG I. L. BELYEA stenciled on the anti-glare panel. USS HANCOCK is lettered on the side of the fuselage indicating the carrier assignment for VF-213 at the time. (National Naval Aviation Museum Collection)

One of VF-213's Demons is seen here on the wooden flight deck of USS HANCOCK, CVA-19. BuNo. 136997 was delivered as an F3H-2N, but by the time this photograph was taken, it had been upgraded to F3H-2 standards, and the N had been deleted from the aircraft's designation in the stenciling on the tail. The squadron's markings included a pale blue fin cap with four gold stars. (National Naval Aviation Museum Collection)

This photo of VF-213's Demons operating aboard USS HANCOCK provides a study of the unit's markings. Note how the walkway on top of each wing is extended back onto the flap and stylized by having its outer edge curve to the outboard tip of the flap. For 307, the last digit of the modex is painted on top of the short beavertail, while on 311, the last two digits are used. The 7 and the 11 are also painted at the top of the white rudder. VF-213 painted a stylized flat black flash aft of the exhaust port on the side of the fuselage to minimize the appearance of streaks. (National Naval Aviation Museum Collection)

This VF-213 F3H-2 is fitted with the Del Mar aerial towed target system which was used for practicing radar intercepts and missile firings. Note that the gun ports have been covered over on this Demon. In some cases, two of the guns were removed from the F3H-2s to lighten the aircraft, and in others, like this one, all four guns were removed, leaving the aircraft armed only with missiles. (National Naval Aviation Museum Collection)

Four Demons from VF-213 fly over the mountains of Southern California. The lead aircraft and the two on the wings are F3H-2s, while the trail aircraft, BuNo. 136978, is an F3H-2N that has been upgraded to F3H-2 standards. It retains the longer beaver tail of the F3H-2N, although it is a bit difficult to see in this picture. The aircraft on the left wing, F3H-2, BuNo. 146740, was the very last Demon built. By the time this photo was taken, the F3H-2 designation had been changed to F-3B, and the F3H-2N had been changed to F-3C. (National Naval Aviation Museum Collection)

Maintenance is performed on the radar of one of VF-213's F3H-2s on the flight deck of USS HANCOCK, CVA-19. Again note that all of the gun ports on these Demons have been covered. (National Naval Aviation Museum Collection)

Right: VF-213's Demons are lined up on the ramp at NAS Miramar, California, shortly before the "Blacklions" transitioned to the F-4B Phantom II. This photograph provides an excellent look at the unit's markings as well as details of the Demon. (National Naval Aviation Museum Collection)

TEST AND EVALUATION SQUADRONS

The Naval Weapons Effects Facility (also known as the Naval Aviation Special Weapons Facility) was responsible for evaluating the effects of naval weapons. It flew a wide variety of U. S. Navy aircraft including this Demon. As was the case with most centers and facilities, markings on its aircraft that identified them with the station were limited to the initials or name of the center on the vertical tail. This F3H-2N has NASWF lettered on its vertical tail, indicating assignment by the Naval Aviation Special Weapons Facility. Another Demon used by the facility had NWEF lettered on its vertical tail. (Artwork by Rock Roszak)

Several examples of each type of military aircraft are assigned to test and evaluation units for a variety of purposes. These include finding ways to improve the design, test system and equipment upgrades, and to develop weapons and evaluate their use with the aircraft. The F3H was no different in this respect, and Demons were assigned to the Naval Air Test Center at Patuxent River, Maryland, the Naval Air Test Facility at Lakehurst, New Jersey, the Naval Weapons Evaluation Facility at Albuquerque, New Mexico, the Naval Missile Center at Point Mugu, California, and the Naval Weapons Center at China Lake, also in California. Test and evaluation squadrons, VX-3 and VX-4, also had Demons in their inventories.

The artwork and photos in this section show Demons assigned to each of these units and facilities, and the captions explain what type of testing and programs went on at each.

The Naval Air Test Center at Patuxent River, Maryland, conducts a wide variety of test programs relating to aircraft and weapons. Demons assigned to the Center were simply identified with the letters NATC on the vertical tail. This is an F3H-2M used to conduct tests with the Sparrow I missile. (U. S. Navy photograph from the collection of Don Spering)

Above: By the time this photo was taken of a Demon assigned to the Naval Missile Center, the designation for the F3H-2N had been changed to F-3C. This is F-3C, BuNo. 133566. It was originally an early F3H-2N in the very first production block of that version. (Photograph from the collection of Don Linn)

Right: Other Demons assigned to the Naval Air Missile Center had POINT MUGU lettered on their vertical tails. Such was the case of this F3H-2M that was used for tests with the Sparrow I missile. (Photo from the collection of Lloyd Jones)

Located at Lakehurst, New Jersey, the Naval Air Test Facility was involved in the development of carrier systems like catapults and arresting gear, and they insured the compatibility of these systems with carrier-borne aircraft. This photo shows an F3H-2M assigned to the NATF. The markings include a red chevron on the vertical tail that is bordered in white and black. NATF is lettered in black below it. (National Naval Aviation Museum)

91

VX-3 was an evaluation squadron tasked with the development of jet fighter tactics and procedures for the Navy. From November 1948 until July 1958, it was located at NAS Atlantic City, New Jersey. It was then moved to NAS Oceana, Virginia, where it remained until it was decommissioned on March 1, 1960. It had several types of Navy fighters in its inventory, including this F3H-2N Demon. (Artwork by Rock Roszak)

VX-4 was originally established at Floyd Bennett Field, New York, on May 15, 1946, and assigned the task of airborne early warning development. In September 1952, it was moved to the Naval Missile Center at Point Mugu, California, and its mission was changed to the development of air-launched guided missiles. During that time, it flew Demons and was part of the program associated with both the Sparrow I and Sparrow III missiles. (Artwork by Rock Roszak)

Flame erupts behind an AAM-N-7A (AIM-9B) Sidewinder missile as it is launched from an F3H-2N assigned to the Naval Weapons Center at China Lake, California. Markings for the Center are limited to CHINA LAKE being lettered on the vertical tail. (National Naval Aviation Museum)

MODELERS SECTION

General Comments

When building a model of the Demon, the modeler must be diligent in insuring the model is accurately represented. Considerable misinformation has been published about the Demon, and the model companies have made some serious mistakes in creating their kits. To even a greater extent than for most other aircraft types, modelers need to research the subject thoroughly and take extra precautions to insure their models are accurate.

Perhaps the biggest problem area has to do with the missile armament. Our look at Demon models entered in contests, up to and including the national level of competition, and a review of completed Demon models on the Internet almost invariably show incorrect missiles and missile rails on models. Further, as will be discussed in the kit reviews below, model companies, particularly Hobby Boss, have provided incorrect launch rails and missiles for the Demon variants.

As a review, the F3H-2M is the only variant that carried the Sparrow I missile and its AERO 3A launcher. The F3H-2M could not employ the Sparrow III missile, so building a model of an F3H-2M with a Sparrow III missile or an AERO 4A launcher would be inaccurate. F3H-2s could carry the Sparrow III missile, as could F3H-2Ns that were upgraded to F3H-2 standards. The F3H-2N, -2M, and -2 could all carry the Sidewinder missile once it became available, but F3H-2Ms were being withdrawn from service by the time the Sidewinder was in widespread use, so it was not seen that often on an F3H-2M. Len Kaine, who flew F3H-2Ms with VF-61, said he does not recall ever seeing a Sidewinder missile on one of their Demons.

Another item that should be watched is which ejection seat is correct for the model being built. Two types were used, and both are illustrated in the Demon Details chapter of this publication. First was the McDonnell seat, and this was initially installed in all Demons except the last block of F3H-2s (BuNos. 146709, and up). The second was the Martin Baker H5 seat. This was installed in the last block of F3H-2s on the production line, and it was quickly retrofitted to existing Demons. Unfortunately, with the exception of the old Rareplanes 1/72nd scale vacuformed kit, not one Demon kit comes with the Martin Baker seat, yet it is the seat found in F3H-2Ns and F3H-2s during most of their operational service. After-market resin seats represent the later Martin Baker H7 seat, but we are not aware of one that is an H5. However, those made for the F-4 Phantom can fairly easily be modified to closely represent the seat used in the Demon. Using a modified resin Martin Baker seat will be far more accurate than using the kit supplied McDonnell seat for many F3H-2N and F3H-2 models.

Whenever possible, the modeler should try to find a photograph of the actual aircraft to be modeled. To determine the correct seat, look for the two face curtain rings high in the canopy. If they are present, the seat is the Martin Baker seat. If there is a handle at the top of the seat on the forward edge rather than the face curtain rings, the seat is the McDonnell product. Photos will also provide a reference for the unit and other markings used on the specific aircraft. Even the "standard" markings varied considerably, so having one or more photographs of the Demon to be modeled will help insure accuracy.

Yet another area to be watched is the landing gear. Some Demons had a landing/taxi light on the nose gear strut, while others did not. On most Demons, the gear struts were white and the inside edges of the gear doors were painted red. But on a few Demons, the struts were silver, and the entire inside surface of each gear door was red. Also pay attention to the use of the wing spoilers. These were added after the Demon entered service, but not very long afterwards. In most cases, Demons had these spoilers. Only F3H-2Ms and F3H-2Ns flew without them, but even then it was for a relatively short period of time. Any model representing a Demon from 1958 on should have the spoilers. Unfortunately, one of the Emhar 1/72nd kits, kit number 3002 which builds the F3H-N and F3H-2M, does not provide the wing spoilers.

Finally, and very important, be sure to use the correct beaver tail. F3H-2Ns and F3H-2Ms had the long beaver tail. F3H-2s had the short beaver tail. Most F3H-2Ns that were upgraded to F3H-2

93

standards retained their long beaver tails, but in a few cases, the short beaver tail did show up on some of the upgraded F3H-2Ns. Here again, a photograph of the actual Demon to be modeled will be helpful.

Where modelers need to be most careful about using the correct beaver tail is with the Hobby Boss kits. Hobby Boss got the beaver tails backwards in their kits. Their kit for the F3H-2M provides the short beaver tail instead of the correct long one, and their kit for the F3H-2 provides the long beaver tail instead of the short one.

As a final general note when modeling the Demon, all Demon kits will require weight in the nose in order for them to sit properly on their landing gear when finished. Some instructions point this out, but others do not. Be sure to add that weight!

The best way to insure the model being built is accurate is to check each feature against the photographs of details found in the Demon Details chapter of this book. But also read and study the text and captions throughout the book. They should prove to be very helpful in assuring accuracy for any Demon model being built.

As of December 2013, only 1/72nd and 1/48th scale plastic model kits of the Demon had been released. Hopefully, a quality 1/32nd scale kit will be offered in the future.

KIT REVIEWS

1/72nd SCALE KITS

For many years, the only kits of the Demon available to modelers were two vacuformed kits in 1/72nd scale. One was by Rareplanes, which was a decent vacuformed model that included white metal landing gear and refueling probe. The other vacuformed Demon was from Airmodel, and it was quite crude and inaccurate. Today, with injected models available, these two vacuformed kits are of interest only to collectors.

As this is written, there are two kits available of the Demon in 1/72nd scale. They are actually the same kit released in two different versions by the British company, Emhar. Both versions of the kit are molded in light gray plastic, are generally accurate in outline, and have engraved panel lines, although the lines are a bit on the heavy side. Overall, the molding of the plastic is generally good, but it is not as crisp and delicate as seen on 1/72nd scale kits from other companies. The large boundary layer fences are molded as part of the wings, but the three small fences on the leading edge of each wing are missing. Also missing are the small air scoops under each wing and the wing tip skids under the wing tips. The speed brakes are solid pieces with no perforations or even dimples to represent the holes that are in the real items. There is no detailing inside the wells for the speed brakes or inside the wheel wells.

Emhar makes the only injection-molded plastic model kit of the Demon in 1/72nd scale. It has been released twice. One kit can be built as an F3H-2N or F3H-2M, and the other release is for the F3H-2 version. (Kinzey)

Emhar left out a lot of obvious details that need to be added by the modeler. The author used the F3H-2 kit to build this model of the CAG aircraft from VF-41. (Kinzey)

Emhar left out a lot of other details that would be rather obvious on the completed model, and these need to be added by the modeler from scratch. In addition to the wing tip skids mentioned above, the upper beacon on the fuselage, white position light on the beaver tail, the deflectors for the shell and link chutes, and the gun camera faring are all missing, but they are easily added from plastic stock and rods. But Emhar also left out all vents. These include the vents on both nose gear doors, the vents for the gun gasses on the forward fuselage, and the vents on either side of the upper fuselage. No representations of the shell and ejector chutes are molded into the plastic. These vents and chutes would be very tedious for a modeler to scribe into place, and Emhar should have included them during the molding of the kit. Also missing are any representation of the antenna panels for the TACAN Lower UHF, IFF, and Radar Altimeter antennas. These are not scribed into the plastic nor are they included as decals. The modeler will have to paint these on or make decals to represent them.

The relatively complex landing gear of the Demon is not well represented, and parts are missing from the nose gear. There is no representation of the long side struts on the nose gear, and there are no approach indicator lights or landing/taxi light. The modeler can use wire, sprue, and plastic card stock to improve the landing gear, and brass parts are available from Airwaves. The detailing on the main gear wheels does not look anything like that on the actual aircraft.

There are six sets of locating holes for pylons under the wings, but the pylons and external stores vary between the two releases of the kit. In both kits, two fuselage pylons are provided, as are two 282-gallon fuel tanks. Fortunately, the tanks are each molded as two parts and are separate from the pylons. This allows the modeler to easily use the pylons but not the tanks if he so chooses. A refueling probe is provided and can be used or left off as the modeler desires.

The cockpit is very basic and has a tub into which a two-piece representation of the McDonnell seat is to be glued. A control column and an instrument panel are also provided. Unfortunately, neither the instrument panel nor the side consoles on the tub have any detailing, and there are no decals to provide the details for these parts.

The canopy and windscreen are two separate parts, so the canopy can be displayed in the open or closed position. While the clear parts are a little on the thick side, they are not overly so except along the sides of the windscreen. There is no representation of the pitot head at the base of the windscreen, and this should be made out of fine wire and added in the correct location. Further, the intake scoop for the radar cooling duct, just forward of the windscreen, is also missing. This will take some skilled plastic surgery to add.

Kit number EM3001 represents an F3H-2. It comes with the short beaver tail, which is correct for this variant of the Demon. In addition to the fuselage pylons and two fuel tanks, four under-wing pylons are provided. Two of these have AERO 1A launchers for Sidewinder missiles, and two have AERO 4A launchers for Sparrow III missiles. The instruction sheet shows the ones with the AERO 4A launch rails going on stations 3 and 6, and the ones with the AERO 1A rails going on stations 1 and 8. While this arrangement was actually used, these could easily be reversed if the modeler wants to use the more common arrangement of having Sidewinders inboard and Sparrow IIIs outboard. There are no pylons or stores for stations 3 and 7, so this means that the modeler will need to fill and sand the two holes for these stations under the wings.

Two Sidewinder and two Sparrow III missiles are provided in the kit. The Sparrow IIIs are marginal, but the Sidewinders are crude and inaccurate. We strongly recommend replacing these with more accurate versions from another 1/72nd scale kit or a weapons set. Far better AIM-9B Sidewinders and Sparrow IIIs can be found in Hasegawa's Aircraft Weapons: III, kit number X72-3.

A very important note with respect to the mounting of missiles should be noted here. As indicated on the stores chart provided in the Pylons, Missile Rails, and External Stores section of the Demon Details chapter of this publication, missiles could be carried only on stations 1, 3, 6, and 8. Yet we have seen pylons with missile rails and missiles mounted on stations 2 and 7, which are the center wing stations. This is incorrect for any Demon variant. So do not use the locating holes for these stations on the Emhar kit for the missiles and their associated pylons and launch rails.

This version of the Emhar kit does come with spoilers for the wings. Unlike the speed brakes, they have the perforations represented as tiny holes. These are best replaced with brass parts from Airwaves, and this will be covered in greater detail below.

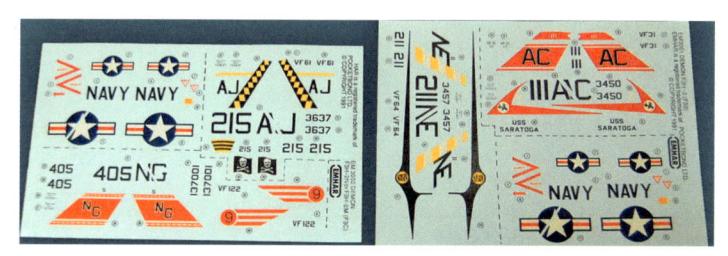

These are the decal sheets that come in the two Emhar kits. To the left is the sheet for the F3H-2N/F3H-2M kit. Markings are provided for an F3H-2N from VF-122 and an F3H-2M from VF-61. Unfortunately, both sets of markings have inaccuracies as explained in the text, and the markings for VF-61 are incomplete, so after-market decals are recommended. At right is the larger sheet that comes in the F3H-2 kit. The markings for VF-31 also have an inaccuracy as explained in the text. Those for VF-64 are better. The standard markings and stenciling on both sheets are not well done, so again, after-market decals are recommended. (Kinzey)

Decals are provided for two F3H-2s. One is BuNo. 143450 from VF-31, and the other is BuNo. 143457 from VF-64. For VF-31, the insignia with Felix the cat should have a yellow disc instead of a white one, and Felix should be black rather than dark gray. Generally, the decals are not printed as sharply as they should be. Kit number EM3002 is billed to represent the F3H-2N or F3H-2M. It has the correct long beaver tail for these two variants. For the most part, it is the same as kit 3001, with different armament. But in addition to having the long beaver tail, another difference is that this kit does not come with the wing spoilers. This is unfortunate, because most F3H-2Ns and F3H-2Ms had the spoilers for most of the time they were in service. This can be corrected using the Airmodel brass kit as explained below.

To complete the F3H-2N, four pylons with rocket pods are provided. The lines separating the bodies of the pods from the front and aft end caps are much too deep and should be filled and sanded if used. One of the pods in our sample kit had a noticeable sink mark that had to be filled and sanded. Interestingly, only four of these pylons with the rocket pods are provided, again leaving the holes for stations 2 and 7 unused. The modeler can fill them in with putty and sand them smooth, or additional pylons can be made from plastic card and appropriate bombs or rocket pods from other kits or weapons sets can be used. It is just odd that Emhar would mold these holes into both versions of their kit but provide nothing to be glued to them in either case.

For the F3H-2M, Emhar provided four pylons with AERO 3A launch rails for Sparrow I missiles. Four Sparrow Is are also included, and they are reasonably good representations of the actual missile. This is the only Demon kit to provide AERO 3A launch rails and Sparrow I missiles for the F3H-2M. It should be noted that the only Demons usually seen with more than one Sparrow I missile were those assigned to test and evaluation units or Demons placed on display for publicity purposes or open houses. Typically, the three operational squadrons that flew F3H-2Ms seldom carried the missile, and when they did, it was usually only one missile for practice firing at a range.

The decals in this kit have serious inaccuracies. For the F3H-2N, markings for VF-122 are provided. However, the fuselage marking is provided with a reddish-orange disc with a black 9, when it should be a black disc with a reddish-orange 9. Markings for the F3H-2M are those of VF-61, but Emhar evidently tried to copy decals used on a Superscale sheet which had several errors. Superscale had shown the aircraft as an F3H-2 and had provided a bureau number of 143637. No such bureau number was ever used on a Demon. Emhar corrected this bureau number to 133637, which is correct for an F3H-2M. However the other mistakes remain. An AJ tail code is provided, indicating the last markings used by VF-61 while flying Demons. Yet the instructions provide yellow and black stripes to go across the back of the canopy as Superscale did. At the time VF-61 used the AJ tail code, the aft end of the canopy was painted yellow and had small black triangles around the edges. The instructions in the kit also say to paint the tips of the wings and stabilators yellow. The tips of the wings and stabilators on the actual aircraft were painted black and had yellow diamonds. A photo of this actual aircraft, F3H-2M, BuNo. 133637, can be found in the F3H-2M section of the Demon Variants chapter of this publication. The markings on the aft end of the canopy are clearly visible and are very different from those provided on the Emhar and Superscale decal sheets. The markings for the wing tips can be found on the last photograph in the VF-61 section of the Demon Squadrons Gallery chapter.

Airwaves makes two brass detailing sets for the Emhar models in 1/72nd scale and we strongly recommend using them with these kits. They will greatly enhance the appearance and accuracy of the completed model. The first is AEC72060, "F3H Demon Interior & Exterior." It has six brass parts to detail the McDonnell seat and sixteen additional parts for the rest of the cockpit. These include the instrument panel, side consoles, and other panels, levers, and the throttle. Missing parts for the nose landing gear are provided, and replacement parts for the nose and main gear, which can be done well in brass but not in plastic in this small size, are also included.

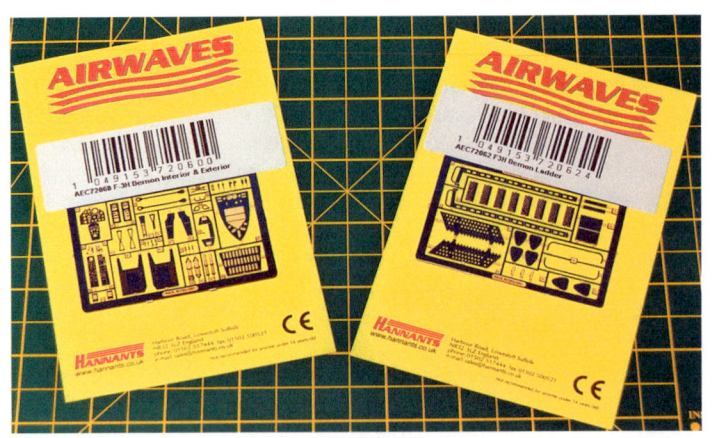

Airwaves makes two etched metal detailing sets for the Emhar Demon kits in 1/72nd scale. Both of these will prove very helpful in providing details that Emhar left out of the kits and for improving some parts that are included. Detail & Scale strongly recommends the use of both of these etched metal sets to any modeler building either of the Emhar kits of the Demon. See the text for more information about what these two sets include. (Kinzey)

Replacement speed brakes are also on this brass set from Airwaves, and these have the scores of tiny holes like the real thing. There is also a cover to go above the rear decking that glues inside the canopy, and the scissors link for the inflight refueling probe is included if the probe is to be displayed in the extended position. Finally, the covers for the upper two 20-mm cannon are also included if the modeler wants to build a Demon that has had its two upper cannons removed.

The second brass set by Airwaves for the Emhar 1/72nd scale Demon kits is item number AEC72062. It provides a boarding ladder, but there are other important parts as well. Most important are the wing spoilers. These are necessary for Emhar kit 3002, which does not have the spoilers at all, but they are also a big improvement over the plastic spoilers provided in kit 3001. The three small wing fences, which are missing from both kits, are also included as brass parts. Finally, there are three small mirrors to go inside the canopy rail, although only two should be used.

The two Emhar Demon kits are now more than twenty years old, and they are not up to the state of the art of today's better kits. But with some patience and use of the Airwaves brass parts, a decent model of the Demon can be built. Until a new Demon kit in 1/72nd scale is released, this is the only injection-molded kit of the F3H available in this popular modeling scale.

1/48th SCALE KITS

Grand Phoenix and AZ Kits

The first Demon model kit to be released in 1/48th scale was by Grand Phoenix in 2004 as kit number 006. It was a limited-production, multi-media kit with parts in plastic, resin, and etched metal. The resin and etched metal parts were produced by Aires specifically for this kit. Masks were also provided to assist with painting the canopy, windscreen, and wheels. The kit was clearly intended for more advanced modelers, and the fact that it was not for beginners is stated on the box. The plastic parts are cleanly molded in medium gray and have nicely engraved panel lines.

The kit is well detailed and generally quite accurate, but it does have several shortcomings. Arguably the biggest of these is the lack of any under-wing pylons or stores, although it does have the fuselage pylons and two 282-gallon fuel tanks. This problem was subsequently corrected to a point when the kit was re-released under the AZ label with pylons and Sparrow III missiles included. Another shortcoming is that it only has the long beaver tail, so it cannot be built as an F3H-2 unless the beaver tail is converted to the short design or a short beaver tail is built from scratch. Converting the long beaver tail as it comes in the kit to a short one should not be too difficult for any modeler who is otherwise advanced enough to build this kit. Since the kit is billed only as an F3H-2N, the long beaver tail is appropriate.

The kit comes with the wing tip skids under the wing tips, which the Hobby Boss models do not have, but for a kit that is otherwise so well detailed, it is surprising to find that the pitot head at the base of the windscreen is missing. Since this is quite noticeable, it will have to be added from scratch. Also missing is any representation of the intake for the radar cooling duct just forward of the windscreen on the nose. This too is noticeable, so some plastic surgery will be required to add it. Finally, the kit comes only with the McDonnell ejection seat, so if the model being built requires the Martin Baker H5 seat, an after-market seat will have to be found and used. However, in fairness, the decals are for two F3H-2Ns from 1957, so the McDonnell seat was probably still used in both aircraft during that early year in the operational service of the Demon. It's just that the option of building a later Demon is not possible without changing the seat.

The instructions are not as good as they should be and contain one major error. The error is that the instructions for both the Grand Phoenix and AZ kits show the wing spar upside down. It should cause the wings to angle down, not up. In general, the instructions should be much better detailed. Modelers need to patiently study the drawings and understand exactly where the parts go before gluing them into place. This is particularly true for the landing gear assemblies. There are no specific instructions as to how to position the in-flight refueling probe, fuel dump masts, and other small parts, so study the photographs in this publication to insure that parts are located correctly. In the AZ kit, the instructions do not clearly show the correct locations for the wing pylons.

Two small bags contain the resin parts, and dozens are provided. The cockpit assembly, many of its detailing parts, ejection seat, wheel wells for all three landing gear, links and struts for the landing gear, the wheels, engine afterburner and nozzle assembly, arresting hook, and small scoops are all provided as resin parts. The speed brakes are resin as well, but unfortunately they only have dimples to represent the multitude of holes in each brake.

The etched metal parts include the main instrument panel, the boundary layer fences, wing spoilers, flame holder to go inside the

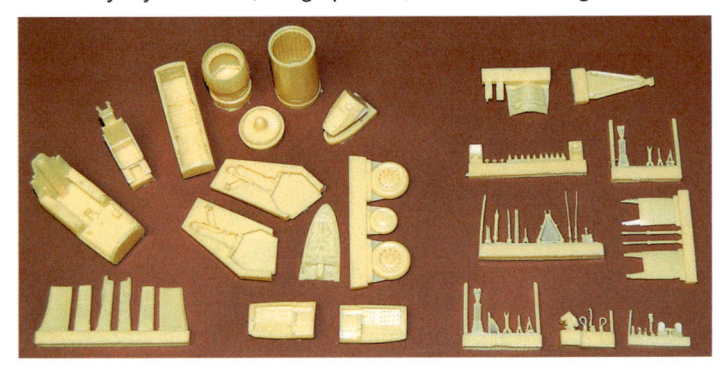

The Grand Phoenix kit has two small plastic bags full of resin parts for detailing their Demon kit. Major components, such as the cockpit tub, seat, afterburner can, and nozzle are among the resin parts, but small detailing parts for the cockpit and landing gear are also provided. (Kinzey)

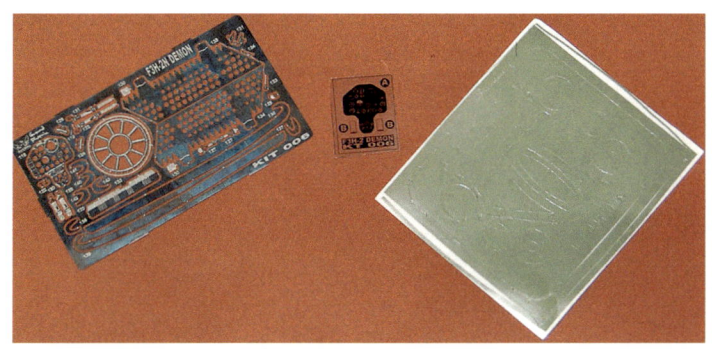

The Grand Phoenix kit also includes etched metal parts, an instrument panel placard, and masks for painting the windscreen, canopy, and wheels. Aires provided both the resin and etched metal parts for this kit. (Kinzey)

afterburner, and small detailing parts for the cockpit and ejection seat. A good deal of patience will be required when working with these parts, many of which are very tiny, but they add super detailing to the finished model. There is also a backing with instruments printed on it to go behind the etched metal instrument panel.

Eagle Strike provided excellent decals for two F3H-2Ns. One is from VF-124 from NAS Miramar, California, that served aboard USS LEXINGTON, CVA-16, in 1957, and the second is an F3H-2N from VF-122 as the squadron deployed aboard USS TICONDEROGA, CVA-14, also in 1957.

Eagle Strike produced the decals in the Grand Phoenix kit, and they are excellent. Markings are provided for two F3H-2Ns, one from VF-122 and the other from VF-124. Both sets of markings are for aircraft as they appeared in 1957, early in the operational service life of the Demon. (Kinzey)

The AZ release adds four wing pylons with AERO 4A launch rails and four AAM-N-6 (AIM-7C) Sparrow III missiles to enhance the Grand Phoenix kit, but AZ did poor research when adding these parts. The problem is that the kit is billed to be an F3H-2M, and decals are only provided for two F3H-2Ms, one from the "Jolly Rogers" of VF-61 and the other from the "Corsairs" of VF-24. The F3H-2M did not carry the AERO 4A launch rails or the Sparrow III missile, so these extra parts are completely inaccurate for the aircraft the kit represents. Although the AERO 4A launch rails and the Sparrow III missiles are not accurate for the F3H-2M, the pylons without the launch rails or missiles could be used for this Demon variant. However, the launch rails are molded together with the pylons, so they will have to be cut off by the modeler. If a modeler wanted to add the correct AERO 3A launch rails and Sparrow I missiles, they would have to be scratchbuilt.

AZ would have been much better off to represent the model as an F3H-2N and provide decals for that variant, because the AERO 4A rails and Sparrow III missiles would be accurate for this version in the later years the Demon was in operational service. A modeler can do this simply by using after-market decals to build an F3H-2N if it is an F3H-2N that had been upgraded to F3H-2 standards. Doing this would mean that the AERO 4A launch rails

Jim Rotramel used the AZ re-release of the Grand Phoenix kit to build this excellent model of an F3H-2M from VF-61. Jim built the model essentially out of the box and used decals that came in the kit. The AZ release is the same as the Grand Phoenix kit with the addition of four under-wing pylons with AERO 4A launch rails and four Sparrow III missiles. Unfortunately, the AERO 4A launch rails and the Sparrow III missiles are not correct for the F3H-2M, and the only markings on the decal sheet are for two F3H-2Ms. Jim left off the incorrect missiles, but the AERO 4A launch rails remain on the pylons. Detail & Scale recommends removing these if an F3H-2M is to be built. Both the AERO 4A launchers and the Sparrow missiles can be used if an F3H-2N or F3H-2 is built instead of an F3H-2M. (Kinzey)

John Fox started with the AZ Demon model in 1/48th scale and added detailing parts from Aires for the open bays to build this beautiful model of an F3H-2 from VF-193 when the squadron operated aboard USS BONHOMME RICHARD, CVA-31. John did the wing fold areas from scratch. More photos of this excellent model and information about how it was built can be found on John's website at www.fox21productions.com/Demon.html. (Fox)

and Sparrow III missiles provided in the AZ kit would be correct, and this is the simplest way to accurately use the launch rails and missiles AZ has provided.

If the beaver tail provided in the kit is modified to the short version to build an F3H-2, the launch rails and Sparrow III missiles that are provided would also be correct. AERO 1A launchers with AIM-9B Sidewinders could be substituted for all three versions, but they would have to come from another kit or a weapons set. Additionally, the pylon to mount the AERO 1A and Sidewinder would have to be shortened in chord over the one used for the AERO 3A and AERO 4A launch rails as provided in the kit.

Hobby Boss Kits

More recently, in 2011, Hobby Boss released two kits of the

97

Demon in 1/48th scale. Unfortunately, they suffer from very poor research and have numerous inaccuracies. To start with, the parts included in each release are not representative of what the kit is stated to be. Kit number 80364 is said to be an F3H-2 Demon, and decals are provided for F3H-2s from VF-31, VF-21, and VF-213. However, the kit only has the long beaver tail used on the F3H-2N and F3H-2M, so none of these F3H-2s can accurately be built using the long beaver tail that is included.

Interestingly, decals are also provided for an F3H-2M from VF-61 with its earliest markings including the E tail code. Hobby Boss tries to pass this off as an F3H-2 by providing that designation on the decals that go on the tail of the model. But VF-61 only flew F3H-2Ms, and the BuNo. provided on the decal sheet is 137033, which is for an F3H-2M, not an F3H-2 that Hobby Boss claims it to be. Using the basic parts in the kit, including the long beaver tail, a model of this aircraft could be built, but none of the Sparrow III missiles or their launch rails could be used, and the F3H-2 designation on the decal sheet would have to be corrected to F3H-2M.

To compound the problem, kit number 80365 is claimed to be an F3H-2M Demon, but it has the short beaver tail only used on the F3H-2! Further, gun ports are only provided for the two lower 20-mm cannons. F3H-2Ms always flew with all four cannons, and they were withdrawn from service before the number was reduced to two on some F3H-2s and F3H-2Ns that had been upgraded to F3H-2 standards after the Sparrow III missiles became operational.

John Loner used the Hobby Boss F3H-2 kit to build this Demon from VF-31. However, the kit only provides the long beaver tail, and this is incorrect for the F3H-2. There are numerous other inaccuracies in the kit that can be seen in this photograph. Most importantly is the fact that the outboard wing pylons are located in the wrong position, closer to the positions for stations 2 and 7 rather than the correct locations for stations 1 and 8. Missiles could not be carried on stations 2 and 7 on the real aircraft. Although both Sidewinder and Sparrow III missiles are provided in the kit, only AERO 4A launch rails are included, and these were used only for Sparrow III missiles. Hobby Boss incorrectly has the Sidewinders being attached to these launch rails, rather than providing the accurate AERO 1A launchers. Also note the oversized and incorrectly shaped deflector next to the chutes for the shells and links. (Kinzey)

The problem with the incorrect variant continues with the decal sheet. Decals are provided for two Demons, but only one is an F3H-2M from VF-112. The other is for an F3H-2 from VF-14, although Hobby Boss erroneously claims this is an F3H-2M and the decals have the F3H-2M designation to go on the tail of the aircraft. It is BuNo. 145288, which is an F3H-2. This is the Demon depicted in error on the box art as well.

Bob Bartolacci used the Hobby Boss F3H-2M kit to build this Demon from VF-112. Again, the inaccuracies of the Hobby Boss kits are apparent in this photograph. Note the short beaver tail, which is incorrect for an F3H-2M. There are only two cannon ports, and all F3H-2Ms had all four cannons during their operational service. The incorrect location of the outboard pylons is visible in this photo again, and the launch rails are the AERO 4A types that were for the Sparrow III missile. Neither the Sparrow III nor the AERO 4A launch rails were used on F3H-2Ms. The beacon is on top of the fin cap, and this feature was not added to Demons until after F3H-2Ms had been withdrawn from service. The static pressure boom on the right wing tip is too short, and the incorrect deflector for the shell and link chutes is also visible. (Kinzey)

Hobby Boss simply did not know one Demon variant from another when producing their kits, and they did not insure that the correct designation went with each bureau number they chose to represent. Evidence of this confusion is indicated by their descriptions of the variants on the sides of each box. They claim that the F3H-2 was the first operational version of the Demon and that the F3H-2N and F3H-2M were improved versions with missile armament. The fact is that the F3H-2N and F3H-2M came before the F3H-2, and the F3H-2 was the most advanced of all Demon variants. They also state that the "improved" F3H-2N and F3H-2M had an increase to four 20-mm cannons, when in fact all three versions were produced with four. Late in the service life of the Demon, the number was reduced to two, not the other way around. Finally, when identifying the two aircraft on the decal sheet with their respective squadrons, Hobby Boss states the Demons are F3H-3Ms. There was no Demon variant with that designation.

To get around these inaccuracies with respect to what variants are represented in the kits, the modeler needs to determine in advance which version of the Demon is to be built. If it is an F3H-2N or F3H-2M, purchase the kit Hobby Boss claims is an F3H-2. That is kit number 80364. If an F3H-2 is to be built, purchase the kit Hobby Boss says is an F3H-2M. This is kit number 80365. It is backwards from how Hobby Boss has labeled the kits, but it will provide the correct basic parts to build the model desired. However, there are still quite a few serious inaccuracies and other problems to overcome once the kit is purchased and the building begins. Both Hobby Boss kits are molded in light gray plastic and have fine engraved panel lines. The surface detailing is quite good. Clear parts include the windscreen, canopy, upper beacon, and the navigation lights for the wing tips and beaver tail. An etched metal sheet provides the wing fences, flame holder, wing spoilers, and speed brakes. But strangely, the metal speed brakes, which have the small holes, are to be glued on to solid plastic parts that cover the holes on the inner surface. The plastic parts should be a framework rather than a solid piece the full size of the speed brake.

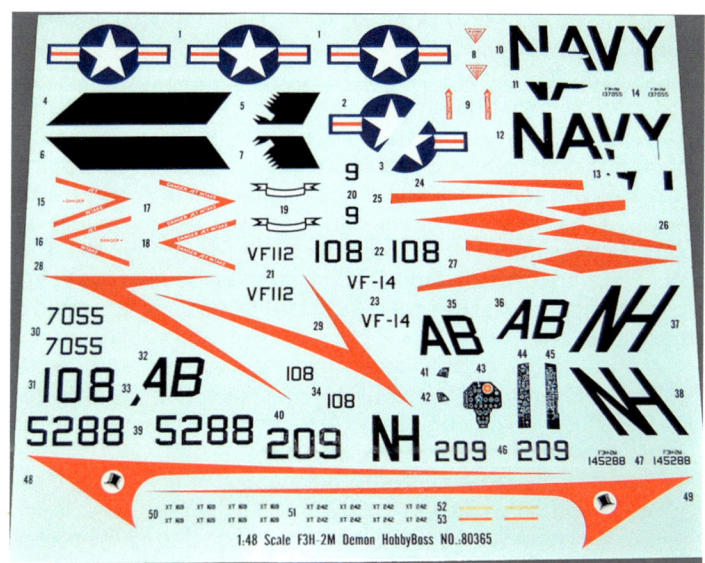

This is the decal sheet that comes in the Hobby Boss F3H-2M kit. Markings are included for an F3H-2M from VF-112, but the kit does not have the correct guns or beaver tail to build an F3H-2M. The other set of markings is for an F3H-2 from VF-14, although the decal sheet and the instructions both incorrectly call it an F3H-2M. It is bureau number 145288, and all Demons with a bureau number that started with 14 were F3H-2s. The kit has the parts to build an F3H-2, but the incorrect location of the outboard pylons will have to be fixed as well as other inaccuracies. (Kinzey)

The biggest and most noticeable inaccuracies involve the wing pylons, missile rails, and missiles, and these apply to both versions of the kits. Two AIM-9B and two Sparrow III missiles are provided, and these are accurate representations of the actual missiles. But Hobby Boss only included four AERO 4A launch rails for use with the Sparrow III missiles. No AERO 1A rails for the Sidewinders are provided, so there is no way to accurately mount the Sidewinders on the model. The instructions say to mount the Sidewinders to the AERO 4A rails, but this would be inaccurate. The modeler is left to find the correct AERO 1A launch rails in another kit or a weapons set if the Sidewinders are to be used.

The second and even more glaring error concerning the under-wing pylons is that the outboard pylons are mounted in the wrong position. It appears that Hobby Boss tried to locate stations 1 and 8 where 2 and 7 should be, but they are not even quite right for stations 2 and 7. Regardless, no type of air-to-air missile could be carried on stations 2 and 7. They could only be carried on stations 1, 3, 6, and 8 as shown in the external stores chart in the Demon Details chapter of this publication. The modeler must correctly relocate the two outboard pylons to their proper positions further out on the wing, just inboard of the wing fold line. These would be stations 1 and 8. Refer to the Pylons, Missile Rails, and External Stores section of the Demon Details chapter in this publication to determine the correct locations for these pylons. The mounting locations for stations 3 and 6 are in their correct position. In addition to the missiles, launch rails, and wing pylons, two fuselage pylons and two 282-gallon external tanks are provided in the kit. In all cases for both wing and fuselage pylons, the mounting holes must be drilled out by the modeler. In the case of the improperly located holes for stations 1 and 2, this is an advantage. Simply do not drill out the holes in the wrong position. Instead drill the holes in the correct position further outboard on the wing.

The kits do provide a pitot head to go at the base of the windscreen, but it is noticeably too large and should be replaced with one that is scratchbuilt to the correct size. The inlet for the radar cooling duct, located just forward of the windscreen on the nose, is represented, and the Hobby Boss kits are the only ones that include this feature. But the wing tip skids are missing. While these small items might be understandably left out of a 1/72nd scale kit, they certainly should be present on one in 1/48th scale.

Another inaccuracy is that the static pressure boom on the right wing tip is too short. Prior to assembling the wings, the modeler must open up the locating hole for the boom. The deflectors next to the shell ejection chutes are considerably oversized and the wrong shape.

In kit 80365, the beacon on top of the fin cap is present in the form of a small bump in the gray plastic. This beacon was added during the last two years of the Demon's operational service, and should not be on any earlier aircraft. It was never installed on any

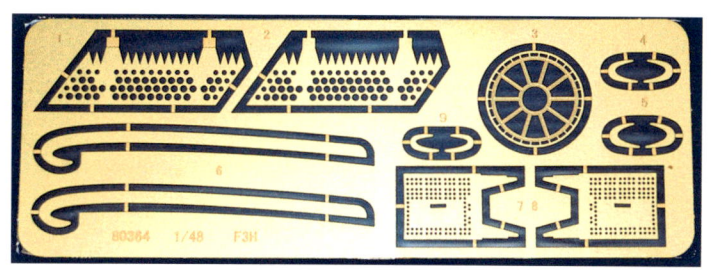

This etched metal sheet is included in both of the Hobby Boss Demon kits. It provides parts including the wing fences, speed brakes, flame holder, and wing spoilers. (Kinzey)

These are the decals that come in the Hobby Boss F3H-2 kit. They include markings for F3H-2s from VF-21, VF-31, and VF-213. The problem is that the parts, specifically the long beaver tail, do not represent an F3H-2. Instead they are for an F3H-2N and F3H-2M. The decal sheet does provide one set of markings for an F3H-2M from VF-61, but the designation on the sheet and the instructions erroneously claim that this aircraft is an F3H-2. (Kinzey)

These two accessories from Eduard will prove helpful for any modeler building the Hobby Boss Demon kits. At left is an etched metal detailing set for the cockpit, and at right is a set of masks to assist with painting the windscreen, canopy, and wheels. (Kinzey)

F3H-2Ms, which Hobby Boss claims this kit to be. Regardless of which variant is being built, if it is not appropriate for the Demon being modeled, it can be easily sanded off.

One nice feature of the Hobby Boss kits is that the wings are designed so that they can be cut along the fold line and then assembled in the folded position. This takes some plastic surgery by the modeler, but the instructions cover making this modification, and extra parts for the wing fold hinges are provided should the modeler decide to use this option.

Unless the Grand Phoenix/AZ kit is re-released or another company releases a new kit of the Demon in 1/48th scale, the Hobby Boss kits remain the only option available to the scale modeler. With all of their problems and inaccuracies resulting from poor research, a good model can still be built of the Demon if the modeler plans ahead and recognizes the problems that need to be fixed. First, make sure to get the kit that actually builds the desired variant rather than what is stated on the box. If an F3H-2N or F3H-2M is to be built, get the kit that claims to be an F3H-2 on the box. This is kit number 80364. If an F3H-2 is to be built, buy the kit that says it is an F3H-2M on the box. This is kit number 80365.

Next, be sure to relocate the outboard pylons for stations 1 and 8 to their correct locations. Once this is done, use the correct missiles for the variant being built, and use the correct launch rail for each type of missile. This will mean finding AERO 1A rails for Sidewinder missiles in another kit or weapons set if the modeler wants to display Sidewinders on the completed model. To display Sparrow I missiles on an F3H-2M model, the AERO 3A launch rails and the Sparrow I missiles will have to be built from scratch. Of course, the modeler can also choose not to have the Sparrow I missiles on the model, thus simplifying the effort to insure accuracy. The Sparrow III missiles and the AERO 4A launch rails that come in the kit are only accurate for the F3H-2 variant and F3H-2Ns that were upgraded to F3H-2 standards. Be sure not to load the Sidewinder missiles on the AERO 4A launch rails as stated on the instructions.

Finally, if the aircraft being modeled represents an aircraft in the later years the Demon was in service, find an after-market Martin Baker ejection seat to replace the McDonnell seat that comes in the kit.

We recommend two modeling accessories from Eduard that are designed to go with the Hobby Boss Demon kits. One is item FE582, which provides etched metal detailing parts for the cockpit. The second item is EX340, which is a set of die-cut masks to assist with painting the windscreen, canopy, and wheels.

Jim Rotramel and Bob Bartolacci contributed to these reviews.

Another view of John Fox's beautifully built rendition of the Hobby Boss F3H-2 from VF-193 is presented here. (Fox)

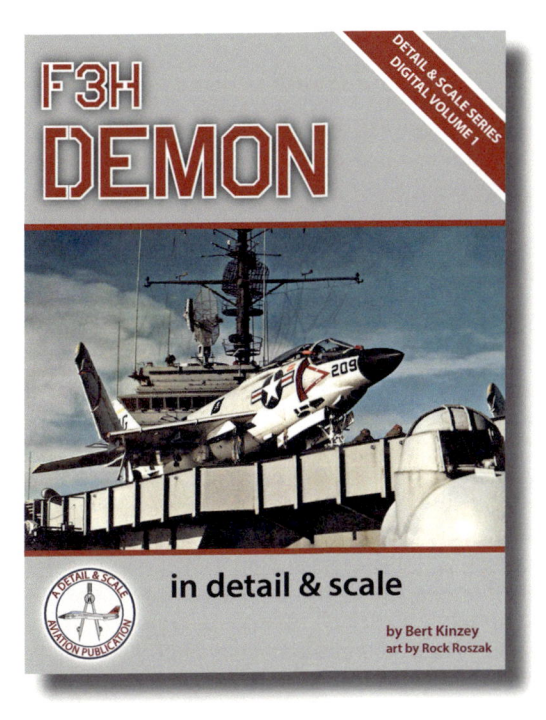

Get the digital version!

The complete book with every high-resolution photograph expandable to full screen on your computer or mobile device, plus all the other great features of digital publications. All for the low price of $12.99.
Visit our website at
www.detailandscale.com
to learn about all of our digital and print publications.

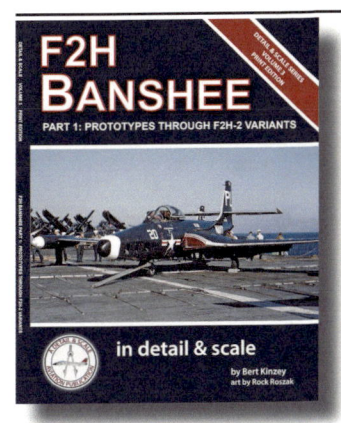

F2H Banshee
in Detail & Scale
$12.99
Print Edition Available!
$19.99

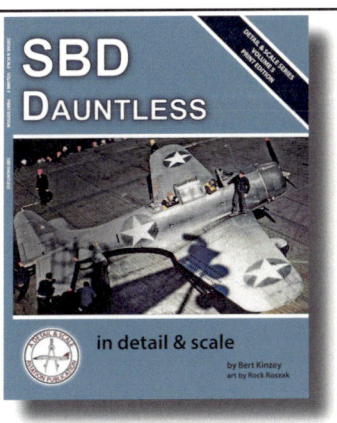

SBD Dauntless
in Detail & Scale
$12.99
Print Edition available!
$19.99

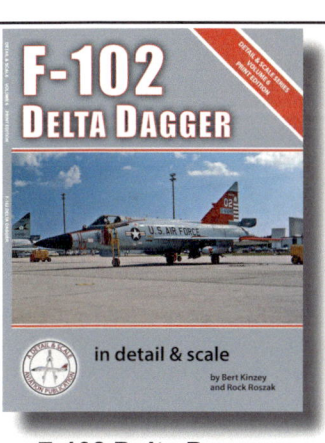

F-102 Delta Dagger
in Detail & Scale
$12.99
Print Edition available!
$19.99

U. S. Navy and Marine
Carrier-Based Aircraft
of World War II
$12.99
Print Edition available!
$21.99

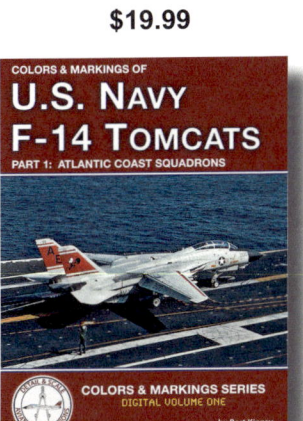

F-14 Tomcat Part 1
Colors & Markings
$12.99

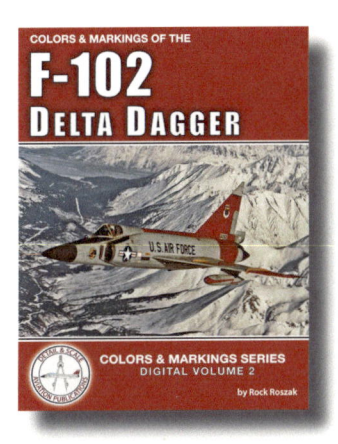

F-102 Delta Dagger
Colors & Markings
$12.99

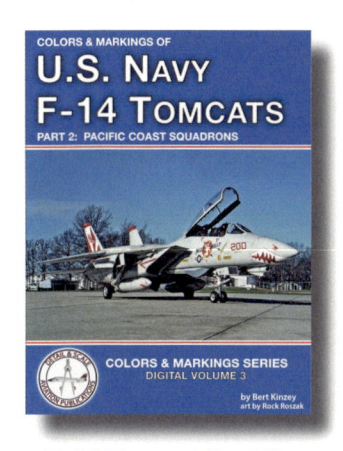

F-14 Tomcat Part 2
Colors & Markings
$12.99

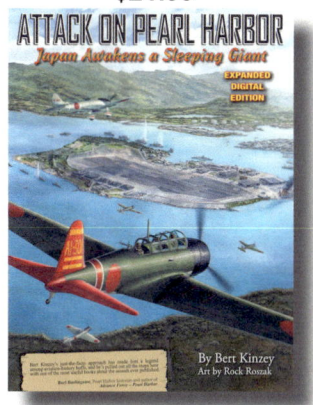

Attack on Pearl Harbor
Japan Awakens a Sleeping Giant
$15.99

ABOUT THE AUTHOR

Author Bert Kinzey graduated from Virginia Tech in 1968 with a degree in Business Administration. Upon graduation, he was commissioned a second lieutenant in the U. S. Army and was sent to the Army's Air Defense School at Fort Bliss, Texas.

During his eight years as an officer, Bert commanded a Hawk guided missile battery just south of the DMZ in Korea. Later he originated, wrote, and taught classes on the air threat, military air power, and air defense suppression at Fort Bliss.

It was during this time that he did his first writing. Bert was dissatisfied with the existing manuals and other materials available for his classes, because they were inaccurate and incomplete. As a result, he wrote his own reference books and other publications. Although he intended for these to be used only in his classes, they were soon placed on the Army's official publication list and distributed throughout the military.

In 1976, Bert resigned from active duty, but his reputation for being knowledgeable about all aspects of military air power soon led to his taking a civilian position as a subject matter expert on the air threat and world airpower with the Department of Defense. His primary responsibility was to develop a new program to teach the proper identification of both friendly and enemy aircraft, so as to insure the destruction of hostile aircraft and the safety of friendly aircraft. This was the first such program in the world to feature dynamic simulation. Bert has also flown with active, Reserve, and National Guard squadrons on training missions to observe the conduct and procedures of air-to-air and air-to-ground combat. As both an officer and a civilian, Bert often briefed military and political leaders of the United States and other nations on subjects related to air power, the air threat, and air defense.

While he was working for the Department of Defense, Bert started Detail & Scale, a part-time business to produce a new series of books on military aircraft. The Detail & Scale Series of publications was the first to focus on the many details of military aircraft to include cockpits, weapon systems, radars and avionics systems, differences between variants, airframe design, and much more. These books became so successful that Bert resigned from his position with the Department of Defense and began writing and producing books full time. Soon, other well-known aviation writers began writing books for the Detail & Scale Series, so Bert became both an author and an editor. Later Bert added aircraft carriers to the Detail & Scale Series, and he also began a second series called Colors & Markings. Each book in this series focused on a specific aircraft type and illustrated the paint schemes and markings of every unit that had flown that aircraft. Bert also produced a book for McGraw-Hill on the Gulf War entitled "The Fury of Desert Storm: The Air Campaign." In January 2002, Bert produced his one-hundredth aviation publication.

Bert has always taken many of the photographs that appear in his Detail & Scale Series publications, and he believes that whenever possible, it is best that the author take photos in order to precisely illustrate what is being discussed in the text and captions. His has also done photography for other books, magazine articles, websites, and for research and publicity that has been provided to clients. He owns one of the most extensive collections of aviation photographs in the world. Over the years, Bert has given numerous presentations and speeches about military air power, the air threat, military aviation history, and aircraft types, working these into his busy schedule of writing, editing, doing research, taking photographs, and consulting.

In June 2004, health issues caused Bert to retire from his work, and his two series of aviation books came to an end. But in 2011, the Detail & Scale website was created at www.detailandscale.com, and a Detail & Scale Facebook page was also begun. By the end of 2013, Bert had completed the first new title in the Detail & Scale Series in almost ten years, and more books were planned. Initially, these new titles were made available in digital formats, but in 2017, printed versions for titles in the Detail & Scale Series were also added. This new venture was made possible through a partnership with Rock Roszak.

Bert currently lives in Blacksburg, Virginia, with his wife Lynda. They have two children and four grandchildren.

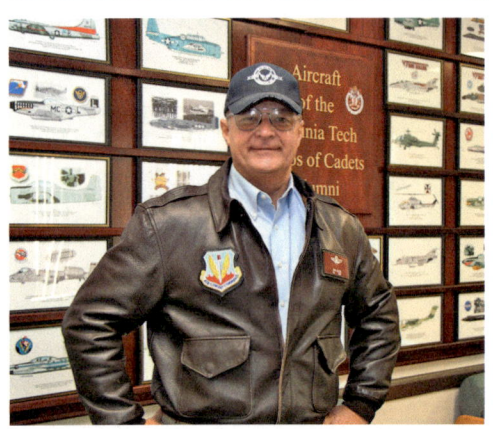

ABOUT THE ILLUSTRATOR

The illustrator, Colonel Richard S. "Rock" Roszak, is the son of immigrants who came to America from a war-ravaged Europe. He grew up in Staunton, Virginia, and graduated from Virginia Tech in 1971 as a member of the Virginia Tech Corps of Cadets. He was commissioned into the United States Air Force where he amassed over 2,000 flying hours, mostly in B-52D/F/G and C-135 aircraft, over a 27-year active duty career. His staff tours included time as a special assistant to the Air Force Chief of Staff, liaison officer for strategic aircraft programs to the House and Senate Armed Services Committees, and as the Senior Technical Advisor to the Special Ambassador for assistance agreements to demilitarize strategic nuclear launch vehicles of the former Soviet Union. His final active duty tour was as the Commander, Air Force ROTC Detachment 875 at Virginia Tech, and during his tenure the detachment led the nation in earned scholarships and grew from the 36th to the 8th largest ROTC unit in the country.

After retiring from the Air Force in 1998, Rock spent 14 years on the staff of the Virginia Tech Corps of Cadets, returning to where he began his military career. During those years he established an alumni aviation gallery, which features his artwork of aircraft flown by cadet grads and highlights more than 60 years of military aviation history. An avid modeler in his younger years, he has been a digital artist for more than fifteen years and has illustrated several books in partnership with his friend, Bert Kinzey. In 2017, Rock's role at Detail & Scale expanded when he authored one book and co-authored another. He is also responsible for converting some of the existing digital Detail & Scale Series books to the new print format.

Rock currently lives in Blacksburg, Virginia, with his wife, Patty, two daughters, and six grandchildren.

Made in the USA
Columbia, SC
04 June 2025